DATE			

A Field Guide to

MUSHROOMS
and Their Relatives

Booth Courtenay

Harold H. Burdsall, Jr.

VNR VAN NOSTRAND REINHOLD COMPANY
New York Cincinnati Toronto London Melbourne

Also by Booth Courtenay (and James H. Zimmerman):
Wildflowers and Weeds

Copyright © 1982 by Van Nostrand Reinhold Company Inc.

Library of Congress Catalog Card Number 80-29152

ISBN 0-442-23118-0 (paper)
ISBN 0-442-23117-2 (cloth)

. Printed in the United States of America

Designed by RFS GRAPHIC DESIGN, INC.

Published by Van Nostrand Reinhold Company Inc.
135 West 50th Street
New York, NY 10020

Van Nostrand Reinhold Publishing
1410 Birchmount Road
Scarborough, Ontario M1P 2E7, Canada

Van Nostrand Reinhold Australia Pty. Ltd.
17 Queen Street
Mitcham, Victoria 3132, Australia

Van Nostrand Reinhold Company Limited
Molly Millars Lane
Wokingham, Berkshire, England

16 15 14 13 12 11 10 9 8 7 6 5 4 3 2 1

Library of Congress Cataloging in Publication Data

Courtenay, Booth.
 A field guide to mushrooms and their relatives.

 Includes index.
 1. Mushrooms—Identification. I. Burdsall,
Harold H., Jr., joint author. II. Title.
QK617.C85   589.2′2   80-29152
ISBN 0-442-23117-2
ISBN 0-442-23118-0 (pbk.)

2

Contents

WARNING

Many species of wild mushrooms are poisonous. Publication of this guide must not be taken as promoting the consumption of wild mushrooms. Both the publisher and the authors assume no responsibility for anyone who does same.

Photography Credits

Veronica Pavlat provided the following photographs:

Amanita brunnescens (page 42), *Cystoderma cinnabarinum* (page 42), *Cantharellus cinnabarinus* (page 46), *Hygrophorus russula* (page 52), *Lactarius subpurpureus* (page 56), *Russula emetica* (page 58), *Inocybe geophylla* (page 78, both photos), *Calocera cornea* (page 104), *Clavariadelphus pistillaris* (page 107), *Sparassis crispa* (page 109), *Sarcoscypha occidentalis* (page 118), *Otidea smithii* (page 119), *Otidea onotica* (page 119), *Bulgaria inquinans* (page 124).

Harry C. Leslie provided the photograph of *Urnula craterium* (page 119).

Most of the other species were photographed by the senior author.

Preface

This book is intended to offer the amateur mushroom hunter a handy volume with which he or she can quickly identify any one of more than 350 species of mushrooms. It is unnecessary to have a background in the study of mushrooms to use this field guide; the illustrated Key for Determining Genus is intended even for those who have never examined a mushroom; and the terminology, chosen with the uninitiated in mind, is easy to follow.

This field guide is meant to serve those interested in identifying mushrooms for the sake of enjoyment. Even though the subject of edibility is addressed here; consumption of wild mushrooms should be undertaken only after careful study and only after an unequivocal determination has been made. Identification of all mushrooms to be eaten should be verified by an experienced mycologist.

Introduction

As all kings are men, but not all men are kings, so all mushrooms are fungi, but not all fungi are mushrooms. When the word "mushroom" is mentioned, most people think of a small object—a fleshy, umbrellalike cap over a more or less central stem—growing on the ground under a tree. For most of us, it is this shape that first arouses our curiosity.

Continued hunting, however, reveals a vast array of shapes and sizes, all quite different in character and appearance. We find the Red Cone with a cap width of one-quarter inch and the Giant Puffball with a diameter of over two feet. There are fungi that look like clubs; others remind us of jelly. Others have pores or teeth instead of gills, and one group has no ornamentation on the spore-bearing surface. In still another group of related fungi the fruit bodies may be cup-shaped or spongelike. Instead of a central stem like that possessed by most mushrooms, some have stems on the side of the cap, but in other cases the body of the fungus may appear as a large, thick shelflike structure, a conk. The variety of sizes and shapes is truly amazing. We find them on a variety of hosts—sometimes even growing from other fungi.

WHAT ARE FUNGI?

All fungi start life from a spore, which is roughly comparable to a seed. A seed, however, is a true embryo and contains all the cells for the full development of the plant: tissue, leaves, flowers, fruit, plus enough food to get it started before it begins manufacturing its own. Usually a spore does not have the capability of producing a whole plant by itself. It is a single cell that, having been dropped by pure chance on a spot suitable for its germination, grows by elongating into new cells. These cells must fuse with cells from another spore of the same species. Once started, the growth is rapid: branching and rebranching, crossing and recrossing, to form a cottony weft of hair-fine threads—the mycelium—in which the contents of both spores are mixed. Hidden in the dark under leaves or debris, growing on bark, trees, the ground, or rotting wood—this is the plant itself. What we see and call a "mushroom" is the fruit. It begins as a small knot of fungus threads that increase in size and become changed into different structures to form a button. The button then expands to become the full-size mushroom. Illustrated is a mushroom that has all the possible structures. However, most mushrooms do not possess all these structures. In some species the ring is not formed: in others the cup is absent, and many have neither cup nor ring. The important part, the spore bearing layer; is always formed on these fruit bodies. It is the mission of the fruit to produce spores for the survival of the species.

Spores, produced by each fruiting body by the hundreds of thousands, are invisible to the naked eye, except in mass. They are so tiny and lightweight that they can be carried by the slightest breeze for tremendous distances. Wind-borne spores may travel around the world and as high as seven miles above the earth. Consequently, many species are not geographically restricted but will be found over wide areas or in scattered areas around the world.

WHEN THEY ARE FOUND

The major fruiting season starts in August and continues until the first killing frost. Morel buffs, however, may believe spring is the only season worth mentioning—Morels are found only in the Spring. Some species, such as the Gray Ink-Cap and the Oyster, may also appear in May and early June, but hunting in June and July is usually less rewarding. A few, such as the Oyster and the Velvet Stem, may be found during warm spells in the winter.

The when and the where of fruiting are both unpredictable. Many factors must be precisely meshed: food already consumed, amount of moisture in the soil or wood and in the air, temperature (the Gray Ink-Cap fruits only in the cool spring and fall, never in hot weather), length of daylight, oxygen content of the air, for some, the season. Other influences are as yet imperfectly understood.

Dry periods will mean few fruits, as will extended soaking rain. Alternating rain and clear weather is the ideal for successful hunting.

Parts of a Mushroom

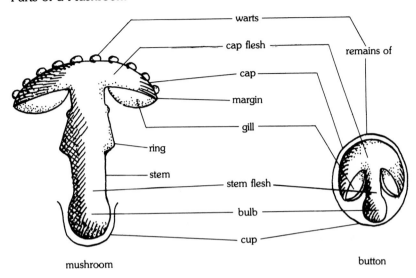

warts

cap flesh

remains of

cap

margin

gill

ring

stem

stem flesh

bulb

cup

mushroom

button

WHERE THEY ARE FOUND

Fungi exist everywhere: desert sands and lake dunes; open fields and meadows; bogs and marsh edges; gardens and farmyards; in or on buildings, lawns, and driveways. But the majority are in conifer (needled) or hardwood (leafy) forests and woods—shady or dark places. For this form of plant life, unlike most others, there is no premium on sunlight. It contains no chlorophyll with which to manufacture food. Like man, fungi depend entirely on other organisms, dead or alive, for sustenance.

WHAT THEY DO

Some fungi are decomposers—they find their nourishment on dead or dying plant material. Decomposers are of vital ecological and economic importance: their disassembling process releases back to the soil, from the host, stored chemicals, proteins, sugars, starches, cellulose, and lignin. Depleted soil nutrients are then constantly re-created and replenished.

It is estimated that each year one acre of forest land is covered by nearly two tons of debris. Without the fungi—the decomposers—to do the clean-up job, our trees would be buried in no time by their own cast-off leaves, twigs, and branches.

Other fungi form mutually beneficial partnerships (mycorrhizae) with the roots of living plants. For example, the northern wild orchids, for at least a part of their life span, are dependent on fungi to make available to them soil nutrients in forms they are able to use; trees also could not flourish without a similar root-fungus association.

Some fungi may seem to be merely mosquitolike nuisances: troops of Glistening Ink-Caps do nothing to improve the appearance of a carefully tended lawn, or the disposition of its owner. Off-setting the disease agents of crop and forest plants are the life savers: *Penicillium,* the original source for penicillin, is one of the most famous of these. And certainly the yeasts are invaluable as leavening and fermentation agents.

Whether fruit of hobgoblins or food for the gods, each of the thousands of fungi has its own niche in the ecosystem, its own specific role to play. All are a source of endless interest to the inquiring mind.

For more in-depth information on the life cycle or biology of mushrooms read *Introductory Mycology* written by C. J. Alexopoulos and C. W. Mims (John Wiley & Sons, Inc., 1979) and *Mycology* written by E. Muller and W. Loeffler and translated by B. Kendrick and F. Barlocher (George Thieme Publishers, 1976).

EDIBILITY

Collecting wild mushrooms to eat may be one way to live off the land—but make sure that you do live through the experience. At the safe end, there are a few whose visible character is so distinctive and unlike any other as to make identification unmistakable, and for which there are no bad records: Puffballs (as long as they are pure white inside), the Shaggy Mane, the Sulphur Shelf, the Morels, and the Large White Coral are examples.

At the other extreme are the poisonous species. Some are killers—especially some *Amanita* and *Galerina* species. Next in line come those that are poisonous but usually not deadly. They are considered as "sickeners" or "dangerous." Among them are the Jack O'Lantern and the False Chanterelle; and (when alcohol is imbibed before, during, or after eating) the Chalk-Top and several of the Ink-Caps. Included also in this group is Green-Gills (the green-spored *Lepiota*), the False Morels, most *Inocybe* species, and the red-pored Boletes. None of these should be sampled.

There are also a vast number that may well have unpleasant consequences for some, though not for others. Analysis proves no poisonous content, but individual sensitivity to particular combinations of elements differs widely; after all, some people are allergic to eggs or milk or even wheat flour. Because no one can predict, before eating, what his or her own reaction will be, you must be keenly aware that trying any mushroom labeled **NOT RECOMMENDED** is taking a calculated risk. Be sure to carefully read and heed the Ten Commandments for Collecting that follow.

Despite old wives' or folk tales, there are no general rules to separate the bad species from the good. Observation precise enough for positive species identification is the path that must be followed. Genus is *not* enough: some *Lepiota* species are edible and choice; others are dangerous or poisonous.

TEN COMMANDMENTS FOR COLLECTING

1. DO take enough time to ascertain the spore color (page 18). Then compare your find carefully with the picture and the word description.
2. DO NOT experiment because it "looks" good. Spore color and relation of gills or tubes to stem, as well as other characteristics must be noted.
3. DO NOT eat any mushroom that does not match the description exactly, in all details. No mushroom field guide can possibly be definitive, and some of your finds may not be included here. So, DO NOT try anything that seems *almost* the same.
4. DO memorize the characteristics of the fatal Amanitas, not forgetting that the basal cup or shaggy bulbous base is often hidden beneath the surface of the ground. DO NOT just snap off the cap. Pull away the soil from around the base to be sure.
5. DO use for collecting: a basket, wax paper, or paper bag (not plastic), and DO keep each different kind separated.
6. DO NOT pick for eating any fungi that are bug-infested or are beginning to rot, dry out, or disintegrate.
7. DO clean off any adhering dirt or foreign matter *before* putting into the basket or sack.
8. DO try only one kind per meal to prevent confusion in knowing the ones to which you may be sensitive.
9. DO remember that, even when certain your find is a species considered edible, there *can* be a personal sensitivity to it which may cause an allergic reaction: eat only a small amount the first time you try it.

10. **DO have your find verified by a person truly knowledgeable in mushrooms, and cook your find as soon as possible after positive identification of a safe species. For example, the delicious Shaggy Mane will turn to black ink overnight—even in the refrigerator.**

GEOGRAPHICAL COVERAGE

No handbook can possibly have room for all the thousands of fungi in the United States: we cover primarily, but not exclusively, those of the Northeastern and Midland sections of our continent. Many of those treated can be found throughout the United States and even into southern Canada. Though many had to be omitted, we include those most frequently found as well as less common, but unusually interesting fungi. The choices represent a broad cross section of the range of fruits to be found, not only those one might be tempted to pick to eat.

To identify species from other parts of the continent or those not treated in this book, the following mushroom books are recommended: *A Guide to Mushrooms and Toadstools* by M. Lange and F. B. Hora (Wm. Collins Sons and Co., Ltd. and E. P. Dutton and Co., Inc., 1963), *Mushrooms of North America,* Revised Edition, by Orson K. Miller, Jr., (E. P. Dutton, 1979); and *A Field Guide to Western Mushrooms* by Alexander H. Smith (University of Michigan Press, 1975). These books are intended for the more experienced mushroom hunter or for one desiring greater depth of information.

NAMES

In all the natural sciences, each different kind of individual has a double name: first *Genus* (example, *Coprinus*), the major subdivision of a family in biological classification, and then *species* (example, *comatus*), particular members of a genus—this is comparable to *Jones, John.*

The beginner may well be confused when different books use different Latin names for the same plant. Older books, perfectly valid for descriptions, can be out-of-date in nomenclature. Modern research techniques and new approaches produce changes in classification, though the fungus itself has not altered its characteristics. For the most part we use the recently accepted binomials from *An Index of Common Fungi of the United States* by Miller and Farr (1975). For clarity, we give some synonyms found in earlier books at the end of the species description and in the index.

While the great majority of birds, for example, have long had at least one "common" name, this is not true of the mushrooms and their relatives. Wherever possible we give an English name: Shaggy Mane for *Coprinus comatus,* Chalk-Top for *Leucoagaricus naucinus,* or Morel for all members of the genus *Morchella.*

Though the technical Latin binomials seem cumbersome to the beginner, the only exact way to specify one's finds or to communicate easily about them is to use the binomials. A bit of practice will make these words familiar and easily remembered.

It has been said that a study of any phase of nature that does not start with biochemistry and end with genetics is nothing more or less than stamp collecting. However, in this particular discipline, mycology, "stamp collecting" is still an important part of the science. In the study of the flowering plants most of the species are known. In mycology, however, this is not the case. Hundreds of species of fungi previously unknown to science are described every year. And many more years will pass before the fungus flora is as well known as that of the higher plants. Without a knowledge of what mushrooms and other fungi are present it is not possible to carry out meaningful ecological research in areas where the fungi are involved, to know what specific organism is causing a disease, or to know what important chemical might be produced by an undiscovered species, etc. Thus, the "stamp collecting" era cannot be eliminated from the study of fungi because too many species are still unknown.

This full-color guide makes it possible to study, with some assurance of accuracy, representatives of the spectrum of Northeastern and Midland continental American fungi.

WHERE TO START

For the beginning mushroom hunter, the best place to start looking for mushrooms and their relatives is at home: in the lawn, in the wooded area at the back of the lot, on the wood pile, or even on a fence post or wooden step. Fungi can be found in all these places. If you notice that mushrooms are suddenly fruiting in your lawn, take a walk to the little woods in the park down the street and look there. If the conditions are right for fruiting in one part of the neighborhood, they are probably right throughout the area. In the woods, however, you will find different species because they are growing in association with trees rather than growing on the organic matter in the lawn. Be sure, though, that your "lawn mushroom" is far enough away from that oak tree that it is not associated with it. If the mushroom is fruiting a good distance away from the outer reaches of the branches, it is probably a "lawn mushroom."

How to Look at
a Mushroom

The easiest way to learn about mushrooms is to go out into the field, find them, and identify them. Compare your find carefully with the illustration; check both the clues in the shared characteristics paragraph and the specific clues. You will soon be able to spot with authority the important clues each mushroom provides, and your repeated experience will make the world of fungi more familiar to you. You will also find your excursions into it more exciting and safer.

DETERMINE THE MAJOR GROUP

This is the first step in identifying your specimen. The Key for Determining Genus on pages 19 to 33 consists of diagrammatic shapes and visible clues to enable you to classify your find as a gilled mushroom, a tubed mushroom, a puffball, and the like.

DETERMINE THE GENUS

Actually, you will be doing this as you are determining the major group. Once you have identified the genus of a mushroom or a mushroom relative, you are more than half way to pinpointing the species. The Key is intended to help speed up your search. It is based on combinations of the visible characteristics described below. Of course, not all of these characteristics will apply to each fungus.

Cap or Body
The key will give you the size range of the *cap* (the fleshy "hat" of a mushroom) or body of the mushroom relative. The size (width) is presented as large (3″ to 12″), small (1″ to 3″), or tiny (¼″ to 1″). You may also find information about how the cap feels—sticky or grainy, for example—or what it looks like as it ages.

Growth Habit

Most mushrooms and their relatives occur in a rather predictable way. For example some species are usually found *singly* (as individuals) rather than *grouped* (in large groups) as other species occur. Still other species are encountered as a number of individuals *scattered* over a somewhat limited area. In a number of species the mushrooms grow so densely that their bases are fused, resulting in groups that are *clumped.* Other types of fungus fruits occur in different ways, especially those found on wood. They may appear as shelves (*shelved*) on the sides of trees or logs. In some cases, especially if they occur on the upper surface of the wood, the body may extend out in all directions from a central point (*rosetted*), or they may even form large numbers of fanlike caps extending up and out from a central stem (*multiple fans*).

Growth Habit of Mushrooms

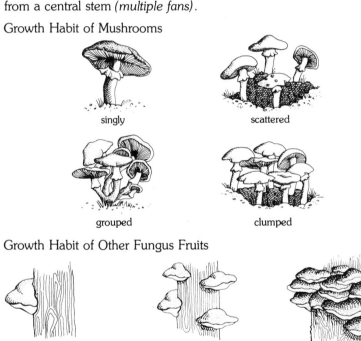

singly

scattered

grouped

clumped

Growth Habit of Other Fungus Fruits

singly

scattered

shelved

rosetted

multiple fans

Gills, Tubes, and Spines

In some mushrooms, the spores are held on *gills*, radiating, vertical plates on the underside of the cap. Other mushrooms have a system of *tubes* in which the spores develop. The underside of the cap of tubed mushrooms has a series of *pores*. These are the tube endings and they may be minute or fairly large. A smaller group of mushroom relatives possesses *spines* hanging from the underside of the cap. In some species they may be up to an inch long, or even more, while in others they are tiny.

Relation of Gills, Tubes, or Spines to Stem

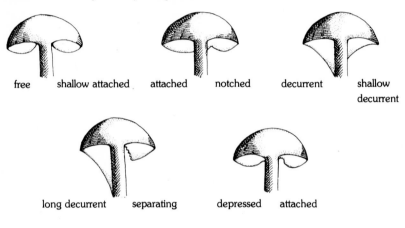

Type of Gill Edge   Pore Appearance

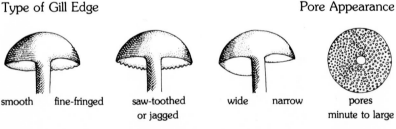

Relation to the Stem

The gills, tubes, or spines are attached to the stem in a variety of ways. Gills may be free, shallow-attached, notched, decurrent (short or long), or separating. Tube attachment is described as free, depressed-free, attached, depressed-attached, or decurrent.

Stem Attachment and Flesh Characters
The relationship of the stem to the cap must also be considered in identifying a mushroom or mushroom relative. The stem may be attached in the middle of the cap (*central*) or more or less off center. In some cases it may be attached, *off to one side (lateral)* of the cap, and in others it is completely lacking *(stem lacking)*. The attachment to the host (usually wood) in these stem-lacking species is at the side of the cap or in some cases the body is pressed (*flattened*) to the underside or to the side of the wood and the upper portion of the body *turned out* away from the host. Other mushroom relatives are merely attached to the underside of their host by the upper surface of their body (*flat on host*).

The *flesh* in mushrooms and other fungi varies in thickness and in color. This is an important character to observe for the identification of some species.

Stem Attachment and Flesh Location

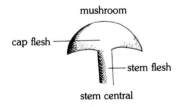

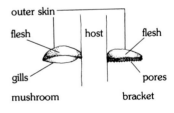

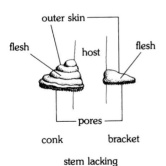

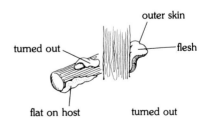

Gill Spacing

When you look at the underside of the cap of a gilled mushroom, you will find the gills in different growth patterns. These patterns include *distant, subdistant, close, crowded, intermediate, forked,* and *fanned.*

Gill Spacing

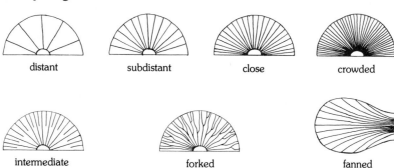

distant	subdistant	close	crowded

intermediate	forked	fanned

Spore Color

The color of the spores is an important clue in identifying your find. To determine spore color, place a section of the cap (gill or pore side down) on smooth white paper and cover with a glass. A few hours or overnight is sufficient time for enough spores to drop. Carefully remove the cup and examine the color.

Silhouette

The sketches in the Key show the typical cap and stem. They also indicate where the fruit is usually found—growing on the ground or on wood. Mention may be made of the growth habit of the mushroom (see page 15).

ground	wood

Key for
Determining Genus

KEY FOR DETERMINING GENUS

In this key, the numbers following the generic names refer to the species descriptions found in the Color Plates and Descriptions section (pages 34–127). They do not refer to book pages.

GILLED MUSHROOMS

White and Pale Spores
AMANITA   1–9
Cap: 1½–12″; dry to slimy
Gills: free or shallow-attached; close or crowded
Stem: with or without ring, base with cup or shaggy bulb (usually underground)

LEPIOTA, CHLOROPHYLLUM (green spores), **LEUCOCOPRINUS, and LEUCOAGARICUS** (smooth top)   **10–20**
Cap: ½–8″; most are scaly, shaggy, or grainy
Gills: free
Stem: ring often loose and moveable

CYSTODERMA 21
Cap: 1–6″; usually grainy
Gills: Shallow-attached or decurrent
Stem: ring often disappears in age

TRICHOLOMOPSIS, LEUCOPAXILLUS, ARMILLARIELLA, MELANOLEUCA, TRICHOLOMA (not shown), RHODOTUS (cream-color spores) 22–28
Cap: 1–6″
Gills: Notched, attached, or shallow-attached
Stem: ring present only in *Armillariella*
Habitat: on soil or wood

CANTHARELLUS, GOMPHUS, CRATERELLUS (no gills) 29–34
Cap: 1½–5″; funnel shape
Gills: decurrent, blunt, forked, distant
Spores: white, yellow, or pink

HYGROPHOROPSIS (white spores), OMPHALOTUS (cream spores), CLITOCYBE (some with flesh-color spores), OMPHALINA, XEROMPHALINA 35–42
Cap: ½–5″
Gills: decurrent, thin, crowded

LACCARIA, HYGROPHORUS (some with cream spores) 43–57
Cap: 1–3″; dry, wet, or sticky
Gills: decurrent or attached, thick, distant

LACTARIUS 58–73
Cap: ½–8″, usually funnel-shaped at least in age
Gills: decurrent or attached, ± distant, with drops of liquid when cut or bruised
Liquid: watery, milky, or colored; often changing color on exposure to air

RUSSULA   74-88
Cap: 1-5″; dry or sticky
Gills: attached or short-decurrent; close or crowded, some intermediate
Spores: white, cream, or yellow

MARASMIUS   89-93
Cap: ¼-2″
Gills: attached or more or less free; subdistant or distant

LYOPHYLLUM, COLLYBIA, FLAMMULINA, OUDEMANSIELLA   94-98
Cap: 1-6″; margin usually inrolled
Gills: attached, shallow-attached or short-decurrent; close

MYCENA   99-104
Cap: ½-1½″; flesh very thin; often in dense clusters
Gills: attached to shallow-attached; distant

LENTINUS, LENTINELLUS   105-110
Cap: 1-6″; often shaggy or grainy
Gills: shallow-attached or decurrent; close; finely toothed on edge
Stem: at side, off center, or lacking

PANUS, PANELLUS   111-113
Cap: ½-6″; tough or leathery
Gills: decurrent or fanned
Stem: at side, off center, or lacking

PLEUROTUS (one with lavender spores), PLEUROCYBELLA   114-118
Cap: 1-7″; fleshy
Gills: decurrent or fanned
Stem: at side, off center, or lacking

SCHIZOPHYLLUM, PLICATUROPSIS   119–120
Cap: ¼–1″; in dense colonies
Gills: fanned; thick
Stem: lacking
Pink, Salmon, and Flesh-Colored Spores

VOLVARIELLA   121–123
Cap: ½–8″; usually silky-hairy
Gills: free; crowded
Stem: cupped at the base
Habitat: wood or soil

PLUTEUS   124–126
Cap: ½–5″
Gills: free, crowded to close

ENTOLOMA, CLITOPILUS   127–130
Cap: ½–6″; most dry, some in clusters, (one looks like a white knotted mass, it is the aborted form of *Entoloma abortiva*)
Gills: shallow-attached, attached or decurrent; sub-distant

LEPTONIA   131–132
Cap: ½–1½″
Gills: shallow-attached, attached, decurrent; sub-distant

PHYLLOTOPSIS   133
Cap: ½–3″; tough
Gills: fanned; close
Stem: lacking

Brown and Cinnamon Spores

CORTINARIUS 134–138
Cap: ¾–6″; sticky or dry; hairy or smooth
Gills: attached or short-decurrent; close to subdistant
Veil: cobwebby, remaining on stem as band of color
Spores: rusty to dark cinnamon

HEBELOMA 139
Cap: 1½–8″; sticky, finely hairy, or smooth, some with cobwebby veil
Gills: free, attached, or decurrent; close to crowded
Spores: rusty to yellow-brown

PHOLIOTA, GYMNOPILUS, ROZITES (not shown) 140–151
Cap: 2–8″; dry or sticky, scaly or grainy
Gills: attached, shallow-attached, short-decurrent; close to crowded
Spores: rusty to yellow-brown or dark to gray-brown

AGROCYBE 152
Cap: ½–3½″; sticky or dry; some with veil
Gills: attached to shallow-attached; close to subdistant
Spores: dark brown

GALERINA, CONOCYBE 153–154
Cap: ½–2½″; sticky to dry; some rounded
Gills: attached to shallow-attached; close to subdistant
Spores: rusty to yellow-brown

INOCYBE 155–158
Cap: ½–3″; usually splitting, hairy or smooth
Gills: free or shallow-attached; close to subdistant
Spores: gray-brown

PAXILLUS 159–160
Cap: 1–6″; dry; velvety
Gills: decurrent; subdistant to close
Stem: central, off center, or lacking
Spores: yellow to yellow-brown

CREPIDOTUS 161–162
Cap: ½–2½″; scaly, velvety, or smooth
Gills: fanned; close to subdistant
Stem: lacking
Spores: yellow-brown to cinnamon

Dark Chocolate, Purple-Brown, and Black Spores

AGARICUS 163–166
Cap: ¾–8″
Gills: free; crowded; pale pink in button stage, becoming chocolate
Spores: dark chocolate

NAEMATOLOMA 168
Cap: ½–3″
Gills: attached; often separating
Stem: occasionally with faint color bands of veil remains
Spores: purple-brown

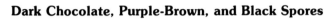

PSATHYRELLA 167, 169
Cap: ¾–3″; becoming flattened in age
Gills: shallow-attached; often separating
Spores: purple-brown

COPRINUS 170–175
Cap: ½–6″ tall; shaggy, grainy, or smooth; quickly turns to black inky liquid
Gills: free; crowded; white at first
Spores: black

PSEUDOCOPRINUS 176
Cap: ¼–1″; does not liquefy
Gills: attached; subdistant
Spores: black

PANAEOLUS   177
Cap: ½–1¼″; smooth
Gills: attached, close to subdistant; often mottled
Spores: black

CHROOGOMPHUS   178–179
Cap: 2–4″; somewhat sticky
Gills: decurrent; distant; thick
Stem: with veil remnants at base of gills
Spores: black or smoky brown

TUBED FUNGI

The Boletes (fleshy)

GYRODON   180
Cap: 1½–5″
Stem: off-center or at side
Tubes: decurrent; almost gill-like
Spores: yellow to yellow-brown

STROBILOMYCES   181
Cap: 2–5″; large, dark, velvety, gray scales;
occasional veil remnants on margin
Stem: dark; shaggy
Tubes: attached
Spores: black

SUILLUS   182–187
Cap: 1–4″; sticky, shiny, dry, scaly or smooth
Stem: with or without ring
Tubes: decurrent or attached
Spores: yellow-brown or cinnamon

BOLETUS   188–189
Cap: 1–6″
Tubes: almost free or depressed-attached
Spores: yellow to olive-brown

LECCINUM 190–191
Cap: 1½–6″; usually white or pale tan
Stem: dotted, tufted, or shaggy
Tubes: depressed-attached or free
Spores: yellow-brown to olive-brown

GYROPORUS 192
Cap: 1–4″; dry, velvety, or grainy
Tubes: free
Spores: yellow

TYLOPILUS 193
Cap: 1½–8½″
Stem: netted in most species
Tubes: depressed-attached
Spores: pink, pink-brown, rusty, or purple-brown

The Polypores (tough and leathery, or hard)

TRAMETES, PIPTOPORUS, TYROMYCES, CLIMACODON 194–197
Flesh: white or whitish
Stem: lacking
Habit: single or scattered

SPONGIPELLIS, CORIOLUS, OXYPORUS, LAETIPORUS, BJERKANDERA, GLOEOPORUS, HIRSCHIOPORUS 198–205
Flesh: white or whitish
Stem: lacking
Habit: shelved or rosetted

BJERKANDERA, POLYPORUS, GLOEOPORUS, HIRSCHIOPORUS 202–205
Flesh: white or whitish
Stem: lateral or turned out
Habit: scattered or shelved

PYCNOPORUS 206–207
Flesh: orange
Stem: lacking or lateral
Habit: scattered or rosetted
Body: orange

GANODERMA, INONOTUS, PHAEOLUS, PHELLINUS, FOMES, FOMITOPSIS, HAPALOPILUS 208, 209, 211–215
Flesh: brown
Stem: lacking
Habit: single, scattered, or shelved

FOMES 212
Flesh: brown
Stem: lacking
Habit: hoofed, scattered

GANODERMA, POLYPORUS, FAVOLUS 216–218, 223, 224
Stem: lateral
Habit: single or scattered
Flesh: white to pale tan
Host: wood

POLYPORUS, FAVOLUS 217, 218, 221–225
Stem: central or nearly so
Habit: single, scattered, or grouped
Flesh: white to whitish
Host: wood

PHAEOLUS, COLTRICIA 210, 226
Stem: central or nearly so
Habit: single, scattered, or grouped
Flesh: brown
Host: ground

GRIFOLA 219–220
Stem: lateral
Habit: multiple fans
Flesh: white or whitish
Host: ground

ANTRODIA, IRPEX, PHELLINUS   227–229
Stem: lacking
Habit: flat on host
Flesh: white to brown
Host: wood

LENZITES, GLOEOPHYLLUM   230–231
Stem: lacking
Habit: single, scattered, shelved, or rosetted
Flesh: white to brown
Pores: as plates, gill-like

DAEDALIA, CERRENA   232–233
Stem: lacking
Habit: single, scattered, or shelved
Flesh: white to pale brown
Pores: as plates, maze-like

THE THELEPHORES (no gills, tubes, or teeth)
(none shown)

CORTICIUM, PENIOPHORA
flat crusts, on wood

STEREUM   235, 237
crusts whose thin edges extend up or out a short
distance

THELEPHORA   238
lobed or fan-shaped, stemless or stemmed

ALEURODISCUS, XYLOBOLUS, PENIOPHORA   234, 236, 239
cup-like or little cushions

CRATERELLUS   33–34
vaselike

JELLY FUNGI *(spores held on all surfaces, occasionally only on lower)*

PSEUDOHYDNUM   240
up to 2″ wide; translucent white, with short spines on underside, on wood

TREMELLA, EXIDIA   241–247
gelatinous or sticky blobs or crowded lobes (flat or tubular) on wood or soil

CALOCERA   248, 250
branched, gelatinous, orange to yellow; up to 2″ tall, on wood

AURICULARIA
tough gelatinous lobed cups, lower surface somewhat veined or ridged; scattered or in crowded colonies on wood

TREMELLODENDRON   249
like a branched club but branches flattened, dense, and tough; white, becoming tan; 1–2″ tall, on soil

DACRYMYCES   251–252
gelatinous sticky blobs, usually orange or yellow, on wood

TOOTHED FUNGI *(spores held on tooth surfaces)*

DENTINUM, HYDNUM, AURISCALPIUM, PHELLODON   253–255, 260
stem central, off-center or on side; on soil, moss, or wood

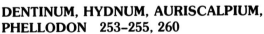
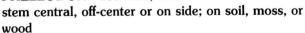

PHLEBIA
flattened, crustlike, warted

HERICIUM 256–258
a mass of interwoven branches from central stalk; all ± white

CLIMACODON, STECCHERINUM (not shown) 259
hoofed, shelved, or petal-lobed. If toothed and jelly-like, see *Pseudohydnum* (241)

CLUB FUNGI (spores held on outer surface)

CLAVARIADELPHUS, CLAVULINOPSIS 261–263
unbranched narrow or broad clubs, some flattened on top; scattered or in dense colonies

CLAVULINA, CLAVICORONA, RAMARIA 264–269
branches delicate, divided or undivided; tips variously shaped

SPARASSIS 270
many thin flat lobes on a thick tough stalk, on buried wood or roots

PUFFBALLS (spores enclosed in tough or papery skin)

CALVATIA, LYCOPERDON, BOVISTA, SCLERODERMA 271–284
outside smooth, hairy, warted, or spined; on wood or soil (see also *Lycogala epidendrum*, 282)

GEASTRUM, ASTRAEUS 285–288
outer skin splits and curves out starlike, exposing a puffball

CRUCIBULUM, CYATHUS 289–290
spores in tiny egglike capsules; "nest" ¼–½″ wide

MUTINUS, PHALLUS, DICTYOPHORA (the
stinkhorns) **291–293**
immature body in a tough egg-shaped case with jelly-
like lining; on wood or soil

*CUP FUNGI (spores in microscopic "sacs" on
exposed surface)*

**ALEURIA, SARCOSCYPHA, SCUTELLINIA,
PEZIZA, URNULA 294–300**
Body more or less cup-shaped, with or without a
stem; on wood or soil

OTIDEA, WYNNEA 301–303
ear-shaped

CHLOROSPLENIUM (blue-green), **CALYCELLA**
(bright yellow) **304–305**
tiny to small cups

MORCHELLA 306–309
top pitted, sponge-like, hollow; cap margin attached
to stem (except in *M. semilibra*)

VERPA 310
top smooth or spongelike; cap margin free, cap
attached only at stem apex; cap up to 1½″ wide

GYROMITRA 311–313
top with convolutions, brainlike, hollow; cap margin attached to the stem or not

HELVELLA 314–318
saddle-shaped or cupped; with or without a stem; some stems are vein-ridged on outside, on soil or wood

SPATHULARIA 319
¾–1½″ tall, tan or yellow, flat ruffle on darker stem

LEOTIA 320–321
caps to ½″; whole body gelatinous; in clusters or colonies on wood or soil

GALIELLA, BULGARIA 322–323
top saucerlike; outside velvety-hairy; inside gelatinous to rubbery

DALDINIA 324
½–1½″ diameter ball; black; layers seen in cross section

APIOSPORINA 325
black gall, encircling twigs and branches of cherry

XYLARIA 326–327
white when young, quickly turning black; inside white, hard

RUSTS *(diseases of living plants)*

GYMNOSPORANGIUM   328
drooping orange strands on Juniper (red cedar)

FUNGI FOUND ON OTHER FUNGI

ASTEROPHORA   329–330
tiny (to ½″) white to tan gilled mushroom on
decaying *Russula* or *Lactarius* species

CORDYCEPS   331–332
small (to 2″) clublike fungus growing on an
underground fungus or insect pupa

HYPOMYCES   333
brilliant orange or red grainy layer covering *Lactarius*
or *Russula* species

PSATHYRELLA   334
brown spores; on aborted-appearing Gray Ink-Cap or
Shaggy Mane

Once you have the genus, go to the Color Plates and Descriptions
section for further details to aid accurate identification. Each large
genus, group of allied genera, and family is headed by a paragraph of
field characteristics normally shared by all. Only those details that
differ from the norm will be mentioned in the species descriptions.
For example, all *Amanita* species have white spores, so spore color is
mentioned only in the shared characteristics paragraph. Most *Lycoperdon* species are found on the ground; if a species is found on wood,
this will be noted in the species description.

Color Plates
and Descriptions

DETERMINE THE SPECIES

The following is a list of the possible details to be found in the species descriptions. Remember, not all of these characteristics will apply to your find.

Common name (when available): Latin binomial.

Cap or body: size (approximate extremes); color (possible variations, changes in aging or from wet to dry weather); surface character (warty, grainy, etc.); attachment to stem, and to its supporting material.

Flesh: color; color change when bruised (if any); other details (when present).

Gills or tubes: relation to stem; spacing; color.

Pore surface: color; size.

Stem: height; other characteristics.

Spores: color of spore print

Growth habit: mushrooms may be found singly, scattered, grouped, clumped, or shelved, etc.

Where found: whether on the ground or on (sometimes under) trees and the like. "Usually" means a chance of another host or habitat; "rarely" means very occasionally found on another host or habitat.

When found: this is mentioned only when it is different from the normal season of midsummer to killing frost.

Role: as a decomposer or in a symbiotic partnership with trees and higher plants.

Other Latin binomials: For variations in nomenclature.

Edibility: The Ten Commandments (see page 11–12) must be followed for each find. We supply the following labels concerning edibility:

EDIBLE: no published record of ill effects
EDIBILITY UNKNOWN: unwise to try; has no positive record
NOT RECOMMENDED: easily confused with dangerous look-alike; too tough or tasteless; too thin or delicate; unpleasant smell or taste
DANGEROUS: known to have ill effects on some individuals
POISONOUS: known to have ill effects on everyone
DEADLY: no proven antidote known

AMANITA CAP: more or less sticky, particularly in wet weather; most have warts or patches which may be brushed off. FLESH: white. GILLS: free; close to crowded; white. RING: above center of stem when present. STEM BASE: bulbous and shaggy-ridged or in a saclike cup; often hidden underground. SPORES: white. They grow singly, scattered, or grouped under conifers and hardwoods with which they all have symbiotic (mutual-benefit) partnerships. Some of the most deadly mushrooms are in this genus. NONE SHOULD BE COLLECTED FOR EATING.

1. DESTROYING ANGEL. *Amanita bisporigera, Amanita verna, Amanita virosa.* Whole body usually pure white. **CAP:** width 2½–6½″; sometimes with yellow or gray tints in middle, usually no warts or patches; margin not grooved, sometimes with ring shreds. **STEM:** height 3½–9″; bulbous base in white basal cup. **RING:** fragile, skirtlike. **DEADLY**

2. CITRINE AMANITA. *Amanita citrina.* **CAP:** width 1¾–3½″; pale lemon yellow to white; patches buff, margin not grooved, often lighter in color. **STEM:** height 1¾–3½″; abruptly bulbous base in cup which may be collared. **RING:** white, skirtlike. **POISONOUS**

3. GEMMED AMANITA. *Amanita gemmata*.
CAP: width ¾–2″; yellow-buff center to cream colored, grooved margin; white warts. **STEM:** height 1¾–3½″; in cup which may age collared. **RING:** fragile, soon disappears. Found on ground or very rotted wood. **POISONOUS**

4. THE PANTHER. *Amanita pantherina*.
CAP: width 2¼–5½″; brown fading to tan or yellow at grooved margin; warts are white and pointed; ring shreds often on margin. **FLESH:** white with tan layer under skin. **GILLS:** fine-fringed. **STEM:** height 2½–5½″; white; smooth above to hairy below ring; base bulbous with cottony cover that easily rubs off. **RING:** white, skirtlike. **POISONOUS**

5. FLY AMANITA. *Amanita muscaria*.
CAP: width 3–12″; vermillion, orange, or yellow; white or yellow warts; grooved margin. **FLESH:** white or pale yellow just below skin. **GILLS:** white, fine-fringed. **RING:** flaring, wart-color. **STEM:** height 4–8″; white, base bulbous with ringlike collar or shaggy ridges; wart-color. **POISONOUS**

6. YELLOW-WART AMANITA
Amanita flavoconia. **CAP:** width 1¼–3½″; yellow to deep orange; yellow warts; margin *not* grooved and lighter in color. **GILLS:** white to pale yellow, fine-fringed. **RING:** thin, yellow. **STEM:** height 2½–4½″; yellow scaled; base abruptly bulbous with powdery yellow flocking often clinging to the soil around it. **POISONOUS**

7. BROWN AMANITA. *Amanita brunnescens.* **CAP:** width 1¼–7″; dark brown, white warts or patches; margin faintly grooved. **FLESH:** white staining red-brown. **GILLS:** white, wide. **RING:** white, fragile. **STEM:** height 1¾–6″; white, hairy below ring; base bulbous split with white veil remains. **POISONOUS**

8. CARVED AMANITA. *Amanita solitaria.* **CAP:** width 3½–6″; white; warts pyramidal, often with reddish brown tips that do not brush off. **GILLS:** white, wide. **STEM:** 3½–7½″; white, very thick; tough stemlike basal bulb deeply embedded in ground. **POISONOUS**

9. TAWNY RINGLESS AMANITA. *Amanita fulva.* **GRAY RINGLESS AMANITA** *Amanita vaginata.* **WHITE RINGLESS AMANITA.** *Amanita alba.* These differ only in cap color. **CAP:** width 1½–4″; patches dirty white; margin long-grooved. **GILLS:** white, fine-fringed. **RING:** lacking. **STEM:** height 3½–4½″; cup large, saclike, white, underground. Found on ground or very rotted wood. (*Amanita inaurata* similar; gray warts on brown-black cap. All are **NOT RECOMMENDED**

LEPIOTA GROUP. *LEPIOTA, CHLOROPHY-LLUM, LEUCOCOPRINUS, LEUCOAGARICUS, CYS-TODERMA.* CAP: with scales or grainy speckles; more solid and persistent in center. FLESH: white. GILLS: free; close to crowded; white. STEM: with ring which may disappear with age. SPORES: white, except dark green-gray on *Chlorophyllum.* Found on ground; all are decomposers of organic litter.

10. SPINY LEPIOTA. *Lepiota acutesquamosa.* **CAP:** width 2¼–5″; white to tan with erect, pointed brown scales; margin often split. **GILLS:** white or pale gray bruising red; edges fine-toothed. **STEM:** height 2½–5″; scaly below fragile ring; base bulbous. Found scattered or grouped on ground or rotted wood. **EDIBLE**

11. BLUSHING LEPIOTA. *Lepiota americana.* **CAP:** width 1¾–7″; white with brown flat scales. **FLESH:** white aging and bruising reddish. **GILLS:** bruise red. **RING:** flares down, soft. **STEM:** height 2½–6″; cap-color, enlarged above base. Found singly or grouped. **EDIBLE**

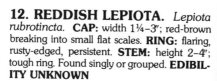

12. REDDISH LEPIOTA. *Lepiota rubrotincta.* **CAP:** width 1¼–3″; red-brown breaking into small flat scales. **RING:** flaring, rusty-edged, persistent. **STEM:** height 2–4″; tough ring. Found singly or grouped. **EDIBILITY UNKNOWN**

13. WOOLLY-STEM LEPIOTA.
Lepiota clypeolaria. **CAP:** width 1–3½″; whitish with small, flat, brown scales; margin grooved or split; edge usually ragged with ring shreds. **GILLS:** fine-fringed on edge. **STEM:** height 1¾–4½″; white; fine-scaly below ring. Found singly or scattered. **DANGEROUS**

14. LITTLE-SCALE LEPIOTA.
Lepiota cristata. **CAP:** width ¾–2″; white; tiny red-brown scales almost absent at margin; unpleasant odor. **GILLS:** edges fine-wavy. **STEM:** height 1–1¾″; white aging pink or rusty; silky below fragile ring. Found scattered or grouped. **DANGEROUS**

15. THE PARASOL. *Lepiota procera.* **CAP:** width 2½–11″; white with concentric red-brown flat scales. **GILLS:** white againg tan. **STEM:** height 5–13′; brown-scaly below flaring movable tan ring. Found scattered or grouped in open woods or grassy places. **EDIBLE**

16. SHAGGY PARASOL. *Lepiota rachodes.* **CAP:** width 2½–6′; white with small, flat, gray-red scales. **FLESH:** white bruising orange-yellow and fading to redbrown. **GILLS:** white staining brown. **RING:** white with red-brown fringed edge. **STEM:** height 4–7′; white; sparsely brown-haired below ring; red-brown at enlarged base. Found scattered or grouped in humus, compost, or mulch piles. **EDIBLE**

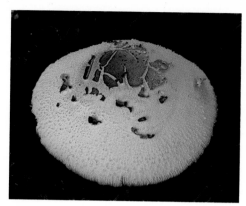

17. GREEN-GILLS. *Chlorophyllum molybdites.* **CAP:** width 3–12″; white with irregular brown flat scales. **GILLS:** white becoming dark greenish-gray. **RING:** prominent, becoming movable. **STEM:** height 3–13″; white or pale tan; base enlarged. **SPORES:** dark greenish-gray. Found scattered or grouped, often in large rings. (Because of its close similarity—particularly when young—to the edible scaly *Lepiota* species, it is *imperative* to check spore color before eating any of them.) **POISONOUS**

18. ONION STEM. *Leucocoprinus cepaestipes.* **CAP:** width 1–3″; white with white (sometimes dark) mealy speckles which brush off. **STEM:** height 2–3½″; white bruising yellow or tan; mealy below fragile ring; base small-bulbed. Found clumped on compost, rotted wood, or enriched soil. **EDIBLE**

19. YELLOW DWARF. *Leucocoprinus birnbaumii.* **CAP:** width ½–1", lemon yellow aging paler; fluffy yellow flocking; margin deeply grooved. **STEM:** height ¾–1¼"; shiny above fragile ring, yellow-flocked below; base bulbous. Found in greenhouses or with potted plants. (Also called *Lepiota lutea.*) **EDIBILITY UNKNOWN**

20. CHALK-TOP. *Leucoagaricus naucinus.* **CAP:** width 1¾–5½"; white aging tannish; surface smooth, not scaly or grainy. **GILLS:** white aging pinkish; edges fine-fringed. **RING:** thick, collarlike, persistent. **STEM:** height 2¼–4½"; smooth, base bulbous, white. Found scattered or grouped. **NOT RECOMMENDED**

21. ORANGE SPECKLE-CAP. *Cystoderma cinnabarinum.* **CAP:** width ½–2¼"; orange-yellow with rusty, mealy speckles. **FLESH:** white with rusty layer under skin. **GILLS:** attached, aging separated. **STEM:** height ¾–1¾"; mealy speckled below fragile ring. Found singly or grouped on ground or rotted wood. **EDIBLE**

TRICHOLOMA GROUP. *TRICHOLOMOP-SIS, ARMILLARIELLA, LEUCOPAXILLUS, MELANO-LEUCA, RHODOTUS.* CAP: dry. FLESH: white. GILLS: attached, notched, or short-decurrent; close to crowded; white. SPORES: white; salmon for Rhodotus. Found on ground. *Tricholoma* and *Leucopaxillus* have symbiotic partnership with trees; the rest are decomposers of wood and organic litter.

22. RED-TUFT. *Tricholomopsis rutilans.* **CAP:** width ¾–6″; brick to wine-red; hairs spread to show yellow flesh beneath. **GILLS:** attached aging notched; yellow; edge fine-ruffled. **STEM:** height 1¾–4½″; yellow with thin reddish hairs; yellow within. Found singly or grouped on conifer wood. **EDIBLE**

23. BROAD-GILLS. *Tricholomopsis platyphylla.* **CAP:** width 2–9″; light or dark gray; some with dark fibers; dry to moist; margin often split or wavy. **GILLS:** shallow-attached to notched; distant to subdistant; very broad; white or gray. **STEM:** height 2½–6¾″; cap-color; smooth or with dark fibers; base may be bulbous. Found singly, scattered, or clumped on rotted wood. **NOT RECOMMENDED**

24. WOOLLY-FOOT GIANT. *Leucopaxillus laterarius.* **CAP:** width 1½–5½″; white to pale pink or pale yellow in center; some low-knobbed; margin lightly grooved. **GILLS;** attached or short-decurrent; white to pale cream. **STEM:** height 1¼–4½″; smooth above; white and woolly at enlarged base. Found singly, scattered, or grouped under hardwoods. Flesh *very* bitter. **NOT RECOMMENDED**

25. STEMMED GIANT. *Leucopaxillus albissimus.* **CAP:** width 1¼–4″; chalk-white; smooth or slightly hairy toward grooved margin. **GILLS:** attached or short-decurrent; white. **STEM:** height 2½–5½″; white or pale tan; smooth or roughened at enlarged base. Found singly or scattered under conifers. (Is bitter, with unpleasant odor.) **NOT RECOMMENDED**

26. HONEY MUSHROOM. *Armillariella mellea.* **CAP:** width 1¾–9″; tan, brown, or yellow; center grainy aging smooth; sticky in wet weather. **FLESH:** white bruising brown. **GILLS:** decurrent; subdistant; white aging burgundy spotted. **RING:** woolly, white, usually with yellow margin; fragile. **STEM:** height 1¾–9″; tan to brown or olive zoned or streaked; often twisted; bruising dark brown. Found densely clumped on above or below-ground dead or dying trees; wood decomposer. **EDIBLE.** *Armillariella tabescens* is a similar species. It is smaller, up to 6″ diam, lacks the ring, and occurs in the southeastern and southern United States

27. MELANOLEUCA ALBO-FLAVIDA.
CAP: width 2¼–5½"; white to light cream-yellow with darker center; smooth; moist. **FLESH:** white. **GILLS:** shallow-attached to separating; crowded; whitish. **STEM:** height 2½–8"; whitish; base bulbous. Found singly, scattered, or clumped under hardwoods and conifers. **EDIBLE**

28. THE TANGERINE.
Rhodotus palmatus. **CAP:** width ¾–2¼"; deep salmon veined like the inside of a tangerine rind. **FLESH:** tan-pink. **GILLS:** attached; close; pink to deep salmon. **STEM:** height ¾–1½"; may be off-center; salmon inside and out. **SPORES:** orange-yellow. Found singly or scattered on dead hardwood. **EDIBILITY UNKNOWN**

CANTHARELLUS GROUP.
CANTHARELLUS, GOMPHUS, and CRATERELLUS. **CAP:** vase or funnel-shaped; dry. **FLESH:** very thin. **GILLS:** decurrent; thick, rounded veinlike; forking; distant. *Craterellus* has no gills. **SPORES:** white. All have symbiotic partnerships with living woody plants; cream or pink. Most are **EDIBLE.**

29. GOLDEN CHANTERELLE.
Cantharellus cibarius. **CAP:** width ¾–5"; bright yellow aging paler; velvety aging smooth; margin wavy. **STEM:** height 1¾–4"; cap-color. Found singly or grouped under hardwoods and conifers. **EDIBLE**

30. VERMILLION CHANTE-RELLE. *Cantharellus cinnabarinus.*
CAP: width ½–2'; orange-red with vein-side lighter; smooth; margin wavy. **STEM:** height ¾–1¾"; cap-color. Found singly or scattered under hardwoods. **EDIBLE**

31. THE TRUMPET. *Cantharellus tubaeformis.* **CAP:** width ½–2'; yellow-brown, brown scaled; vein-side gray-yellow or orange; margin turned down. **STEM:** height ¾–2'; gray-orange; furrowed. Found scattered, grouped, or clumped on damp soil or very rotted wood. **NOT RECOMMENDED**

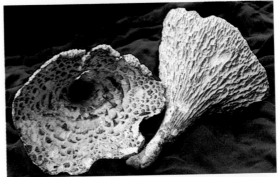

32. SCALY FUNNEL. *Gomphus floccosus.* **BODY:** width at top ¾–3½' (or more); height 2½–8'; yellow-tan to dull orange aging brown-scaled; very young top saucerlike becoming deep-funneled. **GILLS:** long-decurrent; rounded veinlike; forking. **SPORES:** yellow-tan. Found singly or grouped under conifers. **POISONOUS**

33. SMOOTH CHANTERELLE. *Craterellus cantharellus.* **CAP:** width 1¾–6"; light yellow to orange; depressed to funnel-shaped; smooth or fine velvety; outside pale cap-color; smooth to wrinkled. **GILLS:** lacking. **STEM:** height 1–4¼"; cream or pale cap-color; often hollow. Found scattered or grouped under hardwoods. **EDIBLE**

34. HORN OF PLENTY. *Craterellus cornucopioides.* **BODY:** width at top ½–2¼"; height ¾–3½'; dark gray-brown turning black; deep funnel; outside lighter; smooth to wrinkled. **STEM:** height ½–1"; brownish gray to purple-gray, hollow. **GILLS:** lacking. Found scattered, grouped, or clumped under hardwoods and conifers. **EDIBLE**

CLITOCYBE GROUP. *HYGROPHOROPSIS, OMPHALOTUS, CLITOCYBE, OMPHALINA, LYOPHYLLUM, XEROMPHALINA.* CAP: most deep or shallow funnels. FLESH: white. GILLS: decurrent; close to crowded. SPORES: white. Most are decomposers of wood or organic litter.

35. FALSE CHANTERELLE. *Hygrophoropsis aurantiaca.* CAP: width 1–4″; orange-yellow to brown-yellow; smooth or velvety; margin aging wavy. FLESH: pale tan to orange-yellow. GILLS: crowded; forking; bright orange. STEM: height 1–4″; pale orange to yellow-brown; velvety. Found singly or grouped on ground or rotted wood. **POISONOUS**

36. JACK O'LANTERN. *Omphalotus olearius.* CAP: width 1¼–6″; occasionally to 10′; bright orange aging paler; flat or depressed, often with shallow central knob; silky. FLESH: white tinged yellow or orange. GILLS: unequally long-decurrent; close; yellow-orange; glow in the dark. STEM: height 2¼–7″; cap color; yellow within. Found densely clumped on stumps or buried roots. Often called *Clitocybe illudens.* **POISONOUS**

37. BLUE-GILLS. *Clitocybe nuda.*
CAP: width 1–6½″; tan tinged lilac at margin or violet fading to tan; smooth. **FLESH:** pale to lilac to gray. **GILLS:** shallow attached; crowded; blue aging pale gray. **STEM:** height 1–3½″; pale lilac with sparse white hairs. **SPORES:** flesh-color. Found singly, grouped, or clumped under hardwoods and conifers. Often called *Lepista nuda.* **EDIBLE**

38. ANISE FUNNEL. *Clitocybe odora.* **CAP:** width 1–5″; greenish blue or gray to almost white; smooth; strong anise odor. **GILLS:** short-decurrent to attached; white or tinged cream or green. **STEM:** height 1–4½″; off-white to white; base white-woolly. Found singly or grouped under hardwoods and conifers. **EDIBLE**

39. THE FUNNEL. *Clitocybe gibba.* **CAP:** width 1½–4½″; red-tan aging paler; silky when dry; margin grooved; deep funnel. **GILLS:** long-decurrent; crowded; many intermediate, split and wavy with age; white or pale cream. **STEM:** height 1–3½″; whitish; white-woolly at enlarged base. Found singly, scattered, or grouped on ground. **EDIBLE**

40. PEAT-MOSS MUSHROOM. *Omphalina gerardiana.* **CAP:** width ½–1″; gray-brown in wet weather, paler in dry; black-mealy dotted; funneled. **GILLS:** decurrent; subdistant; white to cream; some forking. **STEM:** height 1½–2½″; dark cap-color; tough-brittle. Found on sphagnum moss or damp ground. **EDIBILITY UNKNOWN**

41. CLUB-FOOT. *Clitocybe clavipes.* **CAP:** width 1½–4½"; drab brown with lighter margin; funnel with central knob; smooth. **GILLS:** long-decurrent; subdistant; white to cream. **STEM:** height 1½–4½"; cap-color; base large-bulbed. Found singly or grouped under conifers and hardwoods. **EDIBLE**

42. GOLDEN TRUMPETS. *Xeromphalina campanella.* **CAP:** width ¼–¾"; golden orange; trumpet-shaped. **FLESH:** thin. **GILLS:** decurrent; distant; veined between; some forking. **STEM:** height 1–2"; often tan-fluffy at base. Found very densely clumped on rotting conifer wood. (*Xeromphalina kauffmanii,* on hardwoods, is identical.) Both are **NOT RECOMMENDED.**

LACCARIA. CAP: convex or with a small abrupt central indentation; margin aging wavy. FLESH: cap-color or paler, usually thin. GILLS: distant; wide; fleshy. STEM: tough, fibrous, cap-color. SPORES: white. Found on ground. This group has a symbiotic partnership with trees.

43. PAINTED-GILL. *Laccaria laccata.* **CAP:** width ½–2"; tan, salmon, or terra cotta. **GILLS:** short-decurrent or notched; cap-color aging scalloped. **STEM:** height 1–4". Found singly, scattered, or clumped under hardwoods and conifers. **EDIBLE**

44. AMETHYST PAINTED-GILL. *Laccaria amethystina.* Similar to *Laccaria laccata.* However, **CAP, STEM,** and **GILLS** are violet. **EDIBLE**

45. LARGE PAINTED-GILL. *Laccaria ochropurpurea.* **CAP:** width 2–6″; tan or gray-tan; no central depression. **GILLS:** short-decurrent to attached; deep violet. **STEM:** height 2–10″; often rough-scaly. **SPORES:** white or pale violet. Found singly, scattered, or grouped under hardwoods and conifers. **EDIBLE**

HYGROPHORUS. CAPS: mostly bright-colored; many are shiny, sticky, or slimy. **GILLS:** distant; triangularly thick next to flesh; appear and feel waxy when crushed. **FLESH:** thin; usually cap-color. **SPORES:** white. Found on ground under hardwoods and conifers; decomposers of organic litter.

46. WAX-GILL. *Hygrophorus cantharellus.* **CAP:** width ¼–1¾″; red to orange-red aging paler; dry; center depressed. **FLESH:** cap-color to yellow. **GILLS:** long-decurrent; pale cap-color. **STEM:** height 1¼–5″; dry; cap-color or paler. Found scattered to grouped on moist ground or very rotted wood. **NOT RECOMMENDED**

47. DEER TRAIL WAX-GILL. *Hygrophorus miniatus.* **CAP:** width ½–2″; vermillion to orange aging paler; velvety; margin grooved; funneled. **GILLS:** attached to short-decurrent; cap-color. **STEM:** height 1–3½″; cap-color or yellow. Found singly or grouped. **NOT RECOMMENDED**

48. RED CONE. *Hygrophorus conicus.* **CAP:** width ¼–2″; brilliant vermillion; sticky; bruising and aging black. **GILLS:** almost free; bright yellow bruising black. **STEM:** height 1½–4½″; ridged and twisted; blackening as cap. Found singly or grouped. *Hygrophorus acuticonicus* is almost indistinguishable but does not stain black on bruising. Both are **DANGEROUS.**

49. VERMILLION WAX-GILL.
Hygrophorus coccineus. **CAP:** width 1–2½"; bright orange-red aging paler; moist. **GILLS:** attached; cap-color; interveined. **STEM:** height 2–3½"; cap-color to yellow at base; often furrowed. Found grouped or scattered. **EDIBLE**

50. SHINING FUNNEL. *Hygrophorus nitidus.* **CAP:** width ½–2"; bright yellow aging to whitish; sticky; shallow funnel; margin grooved. **GILLS:** decurrent; yellow, not fading. **STEM:** height 1–4"; cap-color and fading; sticky. Found scattered or grouped on moist ground. **EDIBILITY UNKNOWN**

51. YELLOW WAX-GILL. *Hygrophorus ceraceus.* **CAP:** width ½–2"; yellow, not fading; sticky. **FLESH:** orange or yellow. **GILLS:** attached to short-decurrent, white, close. **STEM:** height 1–1½"; pale yellow within. Found scattered on moss and soil. **EDIBLE**

52. *Hygrophorus chlorophanus.* **CAP:** width 1–1½"; lemon to golden yellow; sticky; margin grooved. **GILLS:** shallow-attached to separating; yellow. **STEM:** height 1½–3½"; sticky. Found scattered, often on moss. **EDIBLE**

53. IVORY WAX-GILL. *Hygrophorus eburneus.* **CAP:** width 1–4″; ivory; sticky; aging shallow-funneled. **GILLS:** decurrent; some forked; separating veins. **STEM:** height 2–9″; sticky or slimy; white-mealy at top to smooth below. Found grouped. **EDIBILITY UNKNOWN**

54. YELLOW GRAINED WAX-GILL. *Hygrophorus chrysodon.* **CAP:** width 1½–3″; white tinged yellow; dry. **FLESH:** white to pale pink. **GILLS:** short-decurrent; white; some forking; separating veins. **STEM:** height 1½–4″; white, yellow-flecked above. Found scattered or grouped. **EDIBLE**

55. HAIRY WAX-CAP. *Hygrophorus russula.* **CAP:** width 3–6″; pink to brown-pink with purple hairs on center; sticky in wet weather. **GILLS:** attached to short-decurrent; close to crowded; cap-color. **STEM:** height 1–3½″; white, streaked cap-color with age; base white woolly. Found scattered or grouped. **EDIBLE**

56. OLIVE WAX-CAP. *Hygrophorus olivaceoalbus.* **CAP:** width 2–4″; dark olive-gray; with thick shiny-sticky coating; aging wrinkled. **FLESH:** white. **GILLS:** attached to decurrent; subdistant to close; whitish. **STEM:** height 1½–3½″; white scaly above aging rusty stained; sticky; curved at deeply embedded base. Found grouped or clumped. **EDIBLE**

57. SOOTY WAX-CAP. *Hygrophorus fuligeneus.* **CAP:** width 1½–5"; black aging dark gray-brown; slimy; convex to flattened; margin pale cap-color. **FLESH:** white. **STEM:** height 1½–4"; slimy in wet weather, white drying pinkish; top grainy. Found grouped under hardwoods and conifers. **NOT RECOMMENDED**

LACTARIUS. CAP: variously colored; continuous with stem. STEM: apt to be short and fairly thick. GILLS: attached to short-decurrent; close to distant. JUICE: all show droplets of liquid when gills are cut or broken. However, in very dry weather or with very old specimens, juice may be absent or scant. This is of special importance in this genus. Juice color—and change, if any, on exposure to air—is necessary for positive species identification. SPORES: white; cream to pale yellow in some. Found on the ground. All have symbiotic partnerships with trees.

58. *Lactarius gerardii.* **CAP:** width 1½–4"; dingy brown; dry; wrinkled; margin often lobed or irregular. **GILLS:** attached to short-decurrent; distant; white. **JUICE:** white; unchanging. **STEM:** height 1–2"; cap-color. Found scattered under hardwoods and conifers. **EDIBLE**

59. SWEET MILK-CAP. *Lactarius subdulcis.* **CAP:** width ¾–2½"; red-brown to red-tan; small central knob; sticky. **FLESH:** white tinged orange. **GILLS:** decurrent; close; flesh-color bruising red. **JUICE:** white; unchanging. **STEM:** height ¾–2'; white above to orange-brown below. Found scattered or grouped under hardwoods and conifers. **NOT RECOMMENDED**

60. RED MILK-CAP. *Lactarius rufus.* **CAP:** width 1¼–5"; red-brown to dark chestnut; broad central knob; dry; silky. **FLESH:** white tinged orange. **GILLS:** decurrent; close; pale yellow to orange. **JUICE:** white; unchanging. **STEM:** height 1½–4½"; salmon; often hairy at base. Found scattered or grouped under conifers. Very similar to *Lactarius subdulcis* but **POISONOUS.**

61. DISTANT-GILLS MILK-CAP. *Lactarius hygrophoroides.* **CAP:** width 1–4½"; yellow to yellow-brown; velvety aging depressed. **FLESH:** whitish. **GILLS:** decurrent; subdistant; white to cream. **JUICE:** white; unchanging. **STEM:** height ¾–2½"; cap-color to clear yellow at base. Found singly or scattered under hardwoods. **EDIBLE**

62. VELVET MILK-CAP. *Lactarius vellereus.* **CAP:** width 2½–5"; whitish; dry velvety; slightly depressed. **GILLS:** attached to short-decurrent; white aging brown-stained. **JUICE:** white; unchanging. **STEM:** height 1"; white; fine-velvety. Found grouped under hardwoods and conifers. **POISONOUS**

63. COTTONY MILK-CAP. *Lactarius deceptivus.* Very similar to *Lactarius vellereus* but with cottony margin. **GILLS:** decurrent; white aging greenish. **EDIBLE**

64. CORAL MILK-CAP. *Lactarius tominosus.* **CAP:** width 2–5″; tan to pale red zoned; sticky; shallow-funneled; margin hairy. **GILLS:** short-decurrent; white or pale yellow becoming red-tinged. **JUICE:** white; unchanging. **STEM:** height 1½–4″; white tinged red, often yellow-spotted; dry. Found scattered or grouped under hardwoods and conifers. **POISONOUS**

65. BITTER MILK-CAP. *Lactarius necator.* **CAP:** width 2–6″; olive-brown with sticky hairs; margin at first olive-yellow becoming pale yellow. **GILLS:** attached to decurrent; tan bruising gray or black. **JUICE:** white; unchanging. **STEM:** height 1½–2″; cap-color; often dark-spotted. **SPORES:** pale yellow-tan. Found singly or grouped under hardwoods and conifers. **NOT RECOMMEND-ED**

66. PEPPERY MILK-CAP. *Lactarius piperatus.* **CAP:** width 2–6″; white; dry; smooth aging deeply depressed. **GILLS:** short-decurrent; white to cream; some forking. **JUICE:** white; unchanging; very peppery to taste. **STEM:** height 1–3″; cap-color; dry; smooth. Found scattered or grouped under hardwoods and conifers. **POISONOUS**

67. BLUE MILK-CAP. *Lactarius indigo.* **CAP:** width 2½–6″; zoned indigo to paler blue, fading to silvery-gray. **FLESH:** blue. **GILLS:** decurrent; blue. **JUICE:** dark blue; slowly changing to dark green, staining flesh and gills dark green. **STEM:** height 1–2½″; cap-color; often spotted. Found scattered. **EDIBLE**

68. YELLOW-JUICE MILK-CAP. *Lactarius chrysorheus.* CAP:
width 2–5″; salmon to tawny; sometimes zoned; depressed. FLESH: whitish staining yellow. GILLS: decurrent; white to flesh-color bruising red-brown; a few forking. JUICE: white; changing to deep yellow. STEM: height 2–3′; whitish to pink bruising brown-purple. Found grouped under hardwoods and conifers. POISONOUS

69. *Lactarius theogalus.* Very similar to *Lactarius chrysorheus.* CAP: tawny red. POISONOUS

70. DELICIOUS MILK-CAP.
Lactarius deliciosus. CAP: width 2–5″; zoned orange to gray-orange or greenish; sticky; depressed. FLESH: light orange. GILLS: decurrent; bright orange. JUICE: orange or saffron yellow; unchanging but staining all parts greenish. STEM: height 1½–4″; dry; orange-yellow aging green-spotted. SPORES: pale yellow. Found scattered or grouped. EDIBLE

71. *Lactarius thyinos.* Similar to *Lactarius deliciosus.* GILLS: long-decurrent; distant. STEM: sticky. EDIBLE

72. WINE MILK-CAP. *Lactarius subpurpureus.* CAP: width 2–4″; zoned dark red and silvery-pink to greenish in age; sticky; smooth. GILLS: attached to short-decurrent; close to subdistant. JUICE: dark red; changing to green; staining all parts green. STEM: height 1¼–3″; dark red, spotted; woolly at base. Found scattered or grouped under hemlocks. EDIBLE

73. LILAC-STAINED MILK-CAP. *Lactarius uvidus.* CAP: width 1–4″; brown-gray to purple-brown tinged lilac; sticky; smooth; depressed; some with shallow knob. GILLS: decurrent; close. JUICE: white; changing to lilac; staining all parts lilac. STEM: height 1¼–2¾″: white at top to purple-gray below; sticky. Found scattered or grouped under conifers. POISONOUS

RUSSULA. CAP: may or may not be sticky; convex aging flat, depressed, or funneled. MARGIN: may or may not be grooved. FLESH: white. STEM: usually stocky and white. SPORES: may be white, cream, or a shade of yellow. Spore color is of special importance for species identification. Found on the ground. All form symbiotic partnerships with trees.

74. SHORT-STEM RUSSULA.

Russula delica. **CAP:** width 3–7½″; white, some with rusty stains; dry; smooth or velvety. **GILLS:** short-decurrent; subdistant; intermediate; a few forking; white or green-edged. **STEM:** height ¾–2½″; may be pale green at top. **SPORES:** white. Found scattered or grouped. **EDIBLE**

75. BLACKENING RUSSULA.

Russula densifolia. **CAP:** width 3–7½″; whitish tinged tan; aging black; dry; depressed. (Flesh, gills, and stem bruise reddish then black.) **GILLS:** shallow-attached; subdistant to distant; intermediate. **STEM:** height ¾–3″; cap-color. **SPORES:** white. Found singly or grouped. **POISONOUS**

76. YELLOW RUSSULA. *Russula*

lutea. **CAP:** width 1–3½″; bright yellow; skin peelable; margin lightly grooved; sticky. **GILLS:** free; subdistant; yellow; interveined. **STEM:** height 1–2½″. **SPORES:** yellow. Found singly. **EDIBLE**

77. STINKING RUSSULA. *Rus-*

sula foetens. **CAP:** width 2½–7″; yellow to tan-yellow; margin peelable and coarsely grooved; sticky in wet weather. **FLESH:** off-white with yellow layer under skin; odor unpleasant. **GILLS:** shallow-attached; close; white aging yellowish; bruising brown; a few forking. **STEM:** height 1–3″; dirty white becoming yellow-stained. **SPORES:** white. Found singly or grouped. **NOT RECOMMENDED**

78. ORANGE-YELLOW RUSSU-LA. *Russula aurantialutea.* CAP: width
2½–7"; yellow to yellow-orange; margin light-ly grooved and peelable; sticky. GILLS: shal-low-attached, separating; subdistant; some forking at stem; interveined. STEM: height 2–4". SPORES: yellow. Found singly or scat-tered. Bitter—NOT RECOMMENDED

79. THE PEACH. *Russula amygda-loides.* CAP: width 1¾–3½"; peach-color
(rosy-tan tinged yellow); skin peelable and very sticky; margin aging deeply grooved. GILLS: shallow-attached; subdistant; white aging bright yellow. STEM: height 1¾–3½"; white or pink-tinged. SPORES: bright or-ange-yellow. Found singly or scattered in woods. EDIBLE

80. THE SICKENER. *Russula emetica.* CAP: width 2–4"; bright red aging
paler; skin peelable; sticky-shiny; margin strongly grooved. FLESH: white with red lay-er under skin. GILLS: attached to free; close to subdistant; white. STEM: height 1½–4"; dirty white. SPORES: white. Found scattered or grouped. POISONOUS

81. NORTHERN RUSSULA. *Rus-sula paludosa.* CAP: width 2½–4½";
blood-red; skin slightly peelable; barely sticky; margin very faintly grooved. FLESH: white with red layer under skin. GILLS: shallow-at-tached; subdistant; interveined; pale yellow. STEM: height 2½–3½"; white tinged red. SPORES: deep yellow. Found singly. EDI-BLE

82. FRAGILE RUSSULA. *Russula fragilis.* CAP: width 1–2½"; rosy to pale red
aging whitish; skin peelable; sticky; margin grooved. FLESH: *not red under skin.* GILLS: shallow-attached; close to crowded. STEM: height 1–2½". SPORES: white. Found scattered. DANGEROUS

83. PURPLE RUSSULA. *Russula xerampelina.* CAP: width 2½–5″; purple to dark red; center dark and often blotched; skin peelable; dry; margin lightly grooved. FLESH: white. GILLS: shallow-attached; subdistant; interveined; some forking; pale yellow. STEM: height 2–3½″; velvety. SPORES: white. Has odor of lobster or crab. Found singly or scattered. EDIBILITY UNKNOWN

84. VELVET RUSSULA. *Russula mariae.* CAP: width 1–4½″; dark purple-red to maroon aging paler; velvety; dry; margin aging grooved. FLESH: all white or with red layer under skin. GILLS: attached; close to subdistant; forking; white aging cream. STEM: height 1½–4½″; rosy or purple-red, may be whitish top and bottom. SPORES: cream-white. Found singly or grouped. EDIBLE

85. THE CHAMELEON. *Russula chamaeleontina.* CAP: width ¾–2½″; shades of red or purple fading to yellow in center; sticky; margin aging lightly grooved. GILLS: almost free; close to crowded; interveined; some forking; yellow. STEM: height ¾–2½″; white; slightly ridged. SPORES: light yellow. Found scattered or grouped. EDIBLE

86. BALSAM RUSSULA. *Russula abietina.* CAP: width ½–1¼″; purple, green-purple, or olive-green with brown center; sticky; peelable; margin grooved. GILLS: almost free; subdistant; white aging yellow. STEM: ½–1½″; white. SPORES: bright yellow. Found grouped under balsam firs. EDIBLE

87. GREEN CRUST. *Russula virescens.* CAP: width 2½–6″; green to gray-green, cracking to show white flesh beneath; dry. GILLS: almost free; close; some intermediate; some forking. STEM: height 1½–3½″; white or pale green. SPORES: white. Found singly or scattered. EDIBLE

88. GREEN RUSSULA. *Russula aeruginea.* **CAP:** width 1½–5″; green with center darker; a bit sticky in wet weather; smooth aging velvety; margin lightly grooved. **FLESH:** white with gray-green layer under skin. **GILLS:** almost free; close to subdistant; interveined; some forking; white aging cream. **STEM:** height 1½–2½″. **SPORES:** pale cream. Found singly or scattered. **EDIBLE**

MARASMIUS. All shrivel somewhat in dry weather and revive in damp or wet; this process may go on throughout the fruiting season. **SPORES:** white. All are decomposers of organic material. Most in this group are too small and thin-fleshed to be of interest as food.

89. FAIRY RING. *Marasmius oreades.* **CAP:** width ¾–2½″; yellow-tan to pale brown aging paler; convex becoming shallow-depressed; margin aging grooved and scalloped, often split. **FLESH:** white. **GILLS:** almost free; distant; wide; ivory. **STEM:** height 1½–3½″; tough; top tan to red-brown; fuzzy at base. **SPORES:** white or tinged tan. Found grouped in rings and arcs in grassy places. **EDIBLE**

90. CLUMPED MARASMIUS. *Marasmius cohaerens.* **CAP:** width ½–1¼″; warm brown aging tan; velvety; bell-shaped. **GILLS:** attached, then separating; wide; close to subdistant; tan, soon brown. **STEM:** height 2–4″; pale cap-color at top, darker below; base white-woolly. Found clumped on ground or rotted wood. **NOT RECOMMENDED**

91. ORANGE PINWHEEL. *Marasmius siccus.* **CAP:** width ½–1¼″; salmon to rusty brown, center darker; lightly grooved. **GILLS:** almost free; distant; white or pale cap-color. **STEM:** height 2–4″; shiny-smooth; white at top to dark brown at base. Found scattered or grouped; attached to fallen leaves and twigs by small white-woolly mat. **NOT RECOMMENDED**

92. *Marasmius delectans.* **CAP:** width ½–2″; ivory drying white; deeply grooved. **GILLS:** shallow-attached; distant; white. **STEM:** height 1½–2½″; top white to dark brown below. Found grouped; attached to fallen leaves and twigs by wide white-woolly mat. **NOT RECOMMENDED**

93. LITTLE WHEEL. *Marasmius rotula.* **CAP:** width ¼–¾″; white; center indented; deeply grooved. **GILLS:** attached to collar at top of stem; very far apart. **STEM:** height 1–2½″; shiny-smooth; threadlike; dark brown to almost black. Found scattered, grouped, or clumped on wood litter, moss, or at base of living trees. **NOT RECOMMENDED**

COLLYBIA GROUP. *LYOPHYLLUM, COLLYBIA, FLAMMULINA, OUDEMANSIELLA.* **CAP: margin down-curved aging flatter. FLESH: white; usually thin. GILLS: attached to free; white. SPORES: white. Found on the ground; they are decomposers of wood and other organic debris.**

94. FRIED CHICKEN. *Lyophyllum decastes.* **CAP:** width 1–6″; white or off-white to gray-tinged; smooth, moist. **FLESH:** pure white; thick in center. **GILLS:** short-decurrent to attached; close; white aging tannish. **STEM:** height 1½–5″; white; solid. Found densely clumped under hardwoods and conifers. Also called *Clitocybe multiceps.* **EDIBLE**

96. PINE-CONE COLLYBIA.

Collybia conigenoides. **CAP:** width to ⅜″; cream or tinged tan; fine-velvety. **GILLS:** almost free; close to subdistant; whitish aging pale yellow. **STEM:** height ¾–1¼″; thread-like. Found attached to cones of white pines by white-woolly hairs. **EDIBILITY UNKNOWN**

95. *Collybia dryophila.* **CAP:** width 1½–3″; tan tinged red or yellow; often with convoluted growths. **GILLS:** shallow-attached; crowded; white or off-white. **STEM:** height 1½–4″; red-brown; base white-woolly. Found grouped or small-clumped, usually under hardwoods. **POISONOUS**

97. VELVET-STEM. *Flammulina velutipes.*

CAP: width 1–4½″; yellowish to red-brown, paler at margin; sticky to slimy; skin peelable. **FLESH:** white or tinged orange. **GILLS:** shallow-attached or notched; close to subdistant; white or yellowish; minutely fringed. **STEM:** height 1½–3½″; pale yellow at top to black-brown below; velvety. Found clumped on dead wood. Grows during fall, mild winters, or very early spring. **EDIBLE**

98. THE ROOTER. *Oudemansiella radicata.*

CAP: width 1½–6″; smoky-tan to brown; sticky; small center knob darker and wrinkled. **GILLS:** shallow-attached; subdistant; very broad. **STEM:** height 2½–10″; white to cap-color below; often twisted; base enlarged then tapering into a long straight "root." Found singly or scattered under hardwoods. **EDIBLE**

MYCENA. CAPS: conical or bell-shaped; when young, pressed flat against stem in a *straight* line (not incurved); margin grooved; not reviving in wet weather. STEMS: thin, delicate. SPORES: white. All are decomposers of wood or organic debris. These cannot be considered edible because of their small size and fragile nature. The members of this group are all **NOT RECOMMENDED.**

99. GOLDEN MYCENA. *Mycena leaiana.* **CAP:** width ½–2″; bright orange fading to yellow; sticky; margin faintly grooved. **GILLS:** attached; close; yellow with red edges bruising orange. **STEM:** height 1½–3½″; all yellow or orange at top; sticky; fine-hairy; yellow-woolly at base. Found densely clumped on rotting wood. **NOT RECOMMENDED**

100. THE BLEEDER. *Mycena haematopa.* **CAP:** width ½–2″; central knob red-brown to paler on grooved margin; white-frosted at first; often scalloped. **FLESH:** bleeds red juice when bruised. **GILLS:** attached; subdistant; staining red; minutely fringed. **STEM:** height 2–5″; bleeds red juice. Found clumped on rotted wood. **NOT RECOMMENDED**

101. PEAKED HAT. *Mycena galericulata.* **CAP:** width ¾–2″; central knob brown to paler at margin; aging silvery; moist but not sticky; grooved to knob. **GILLS:** attached or shallow-attached; distant; dull white, aging grayish flesh-color; minutely fringed. **STEM:** height 1–5″; brown to paler at top; base smooth. Found densely clumped on rotting wood. **NOT RECOMMENDED**

102. *Mycena elegantula.* Similar to *Mycena galericulata.* **CAP:** black-brown to red-brown. Found only on rotted conifer wood. **NOT RECOMMENDED**

103. ACRID MYCENA. *Mycena alcalina.* **CAP:** width ¼–1½″; gray-purple aging pale gray; center darker; acrid odor very strong when bruised. **GILLS:** attached; distant; cap-color. **STEM:** height 1½–3½″; cap-color. Found scattered, grouped, or clumped on rotting conifers. **NOT RECOMMENDED**

104. BARK MYCENA. *Mycena corticola.* **CAP:** width ¼–½″; purple-black aging brown-gray; tiny central indentation; grooved to center. **GILLS:** attached; distant; pale cap-color. **STEM:** height ½–¾″; pale cap-color; smooth or velvety. Found scattered or grouped on bark of living trees. **NOT RECOMMENDED**

LENTINUS, LENTINELLUS. CAP: very tough and leathery. FLESH: white or off-white. GILLS: edges saw-toothed or jagged. SPORES: white. All are decomposers of dead wood, and are found on buried or above-ground wood. They are considered nonpoisonous; but, because of toughness and, in some, bitterness, they are **NOT RECOMMENDED.**

105. TRAIN WRECKER. *Lentinus lepideus.* **CAP:** width 2–6″; tan with coarse, flat, red-brown scales; sticky when young; edge often split. **GILLS:** decurrent; close to subdistant; white to yellow, often rusty-stained; **STEM:** height 1–3½″; white or cream with brown scales below ring. **RING:** fragile and soon disappears. Found singly, grouped, or clumped, usually on conifers. **NOT RECOMMENDED**

106. THE TIGER. *Lentinus tigrinus.*
CAP: width 1–3″; tan with dark brown or black hairs; flat with a central depressed knob; margin wavy. **GILLS:** decurrent; close; white. **STEM:** height ½–1½″; tan with dark hairy scales. Found singly or clumped; usually on hardwoods. **NOT RECOMMENDED**

107. FURROWED LENTINUS. *Lentinus sulcatus.* **CAP:** width ½–1″; white covered with tiny reddish-brown scales; margin furrowed. **GILLS:** attached; white. **STEM:** height ½–¾″; central, paler than cap. Found grouped on wood, especially conifers. **NOT RECOMMENDED**

108. THE FOX. *Lentinellus vulpinus.* **CAP:** width 1–7″; white to cream; coarse-hairy; radially furrowed. **GILLS:** fanning; crowded; white to pale tan. **STEM:** very short, nearly lacking, fused. Found in dense shelving clusters on fallen hardwoods and conifers. **NOT RECOMMENDED**

109. THE BEAR. *Lentinellus ursinus.* **CAP:** width ½–2″; pale red-brown; fine-velvety to smooth. **GILLS:** fanning; white to pale tan. **STEM:** lacking. Found in shelving clusters on fallen hardwoods and conifers. Similar to *Lentinellus vulpinus.* **NOT RECOMMENDED**

110. COCKLE SHELL. *Lentinellus cochleatus.* **CAP:** width 1–3½"; tan to red-brown; irregular deep funnels; smooth or with short erect scales; margin lobed, often split or grooved. **GILLS:** long-decurrent; close; whiteaging flesh-color. **STEM:** height 1½–3½"; central or off-center; furrowed; top flesh-color to brown below. Found in dense clumps on fallen hardwoods and conifers. **NOT RECOMMENDED**

PANUS, PANELLUS. **STEM:** very short or almost lacking. **GILLS:** edges not saw-toothed. **SPORES:** white. Found mostly on fallen hardwoods and conifers which they decompose. *Most* are considered nonpoisonous; but, because of toughness, they are **NOT RECOMMENDED.**

111. ROUGH FAN. *Panus rudis.* **CAP:** width 1–2½"; tan to red-brown; densely covered with stiff woolly hairs; may be funnel-shaped. **GILLS:** fanning; crowded; tan. **STEM:** at side, stubby; hairy; cap-color. Found densely clumped. **NOT RECOMMENDED**

112. LITTLE OLIVE. *Panellus serotinus.* **CAP:** width 1–3"; olive-green or olive-brown; fan- or kidney-shaped; sticky; velvety or smooth. **GILLS:** fanning; close; yellow-tan or pink-tan. **STEM:** a yellow stub at side; velvety or brown-dotted. Found singly or in shelving clumps. **NOT RECOMMENDED**

113. BITTER PANELLUS. *Panellus stipticus.* **CAP:** ½–1"; rust-tan aging paler; fuzzy-scaly, shell- to kidney-shaped; margin often lobed. **GILLS:** fanning; close to crowded; cap-color. **STEM:** flat mealy stub. When young and moist, all parts glow in the dark. Found in shelving clumps. **POISONOUS**

PLEUROTUS, PLEUROCYBELLA. CAP:
white or off-white. FLESH: white; not tough. STEM: short or lacking. SPORES: usually white. Decomposers of dead wood.

114. ANGEL WINGS. *Pleurocybella porrigens.* **CAP:** width ½–3″; fan- or petal-shaped; smooth at margin to fuzzy at point of attachment; often lobed. **GILLS:** fanning; crowded; white becoming creamy. **STEM:** lacking. Found in shelving clumps on conifers and hardwoods. **EDIBILITY UNKNOWN**

116. SAVORY OYSTER. *Pleurotus sapidus.* **CAP:** width 2–8″; fan- or shell-shaped, or (as here) circular with a central stem; smooth; margin aging wavy. **GILLS:** fanning when stem is lacking, decurrent when it is present; close to subdistant. **STEM:** short and stout, may be lacking. **SPORES:** pale lavender. Found scattered or grouped on live or dead hardwoods. **EDIBLE**

117. THE OYSTER. *Pleurotus ostreatus.* **CAP:** width 1–10″; white aging pink or tan; shell-shaped; smooth; moist; margin often scalloped. **GILLS:** fanning; close to subdistant; white. **STEM:** very short or lacking; stocky; fuzzy. **SPORES:** white. Found singly or in dense overlapping clumps on aspen. **EDIBLE**

115. ELM OYSTER. *Pleurotus ulmarius.* **CAP:** width 2–6″; white to tannish aging darker; shape irregular when stem is off-center, about circular when stem is central. **GILLS:** shallow-attached or notched; close to subdistant. **STEM:** height 1–3″; stout; top velvety to smooth, bulbous at base. Found singly or grouped on dead or living hardwoods. (*Pleurotus elongatipes* similar. **CAP:** tan and mottled. **STEM:** top white and cottony. Both are **EDIBLE.**

118. DWARF OYSTER. *Pleurotus candidissimus.* **CAP:** width to 1″; chalky white; fan- or shell-shaped; smooth. **GILLS:** fanning; subdistant to distant; cream-white. **STEM:** lacking or very short; white-woolly base. Found scattered on hardwoods and hemlocks. **EDIBILITY UNKNOWN**

SCHIZOPHYLLUM, PLICATUROPSIS.

Both shrink and are brittle in dry weather, expand and become leathery in wet. GILLS: fanning. STEM: lacking. SPORES: white. Both are decomposers of wood. Too small and tough to be edible.

119. SPLIT-GILL. *Schizophyllum commune.* **CAP:** width ½–1½″; gray in wet weather to white in dry; densely fine-hairy; irregular lobed fan; margin rolled back onto gills. **GILLS:** gray to white; double, separating in wet weather and closing in dry. Found scattered or in crowded groups on live or dead hardwoods. **NOT RECOMMENDED**

120. LITTLE CURLS. *Plicaturopsis crispa.* **CAP:** ½–1½″; zoned tan to red-brown; velvety; irregularly lobed and wavy. **GILLS:** white; not double; ruffled; almost completely covered by rolled-over cap in dry weather. Found scattered to densely grouped on hardwoods, especially alder and birch. **NOT RECOMMENDED**

VOLVARIELLA. CAP: silky-hairy. FLESH: usually white; aging mushy. GILLS: free; white aging pink. STEMS: in a basal CUP. SPORES: pink. Decomposers of wood or other organic debris.

121. ERMINE CLOAK. *Volvariella bombycina.* **CAP:** width 2–10″; white with shiny, silky threads; oval to bell-shaped. **GILLS:** crowded. **STEM:** height 2½–10″; white basal cup large, tan, sticky, tough. Found singly or scattered on living or dead hardwoods. **EDIBLE**

122. SOOTY CLOAK. *Volvariella volvacea.* **CAP:** width 2¼–6″; gray to dark gray with sooty hairs, paler at margin; knobbed. **FLESH:** white or pale tan. **GILLS:** close, many intermediate; rosy aging rusty. **STEM:** 1¾–5″; white; lightly ridged vertically; base enlarged. **CUP:** whitish; margin lobed. Found singly or scattered on ground or compost. **EDIBLE**

123. LITTLE ERMINE CLOAK. *Volvariella pusilla.* **CAP:** width to ¾″; white; silk threaded; bell-shaped aging flat; margin lightly grooved. **GILLS:** close to subdistant. **STEM:** height 1–1½″; dull, white. **CUP:** 3- or 4-lobed. Found singly or scattered on ground. **EDIBILITY UNKNOWN**

PLUTEUS FLESH: white; soon becoming mushy. GILLS: free; close to crowded. SPORES: shades of flesh-color. Found on rotting wood or wood debris of conifers and hardwood which they decompose.

124. THE FAWN. *Pluteus cervinus.* **CAP:** width 2–7″; dark gray-brown aging paler; shiny, moist or sticky; center brown-thready to smooth at margin. **GILLS:** close; white aging spore-color. **STEM:** height 2–6″; whitish to drab; white-thready. **SPORES:** brownish flesh-color. Found singly, scattered, or clumped. **EDIBLE**

125. YELLOW PLUTEUS. *Pluteus admirabilis.* **CAP:** width ½–2″; deep yellow, often olive-tinged; center low-knobbed and a bit wrinkled; margin grooved in wet weather. **GILLS:** pale yellow aging spore-color. **STEM:** height 1–3″; light yellow; smooth; often split. **SPORES:** pinkish flesh-color. Found scattered or grouped. **NOT RECOMMENDED**

126. VERMILLION PLUTEUS. *Pluteus aurantiorugosus.* **CAP:** width 1–2″; yellow-orange to vermillion on knob; smooth or fine-grainy; margin often split. **GILLS:** subdistant; white aging pink-tan. **STEM:** height 1¼–2½″; yellow to orange at base; thready-furrowed. **SPORES:** pink-tan. Found singly, grouped, or clumped. **EDIBILITY UNKNOWN**

ENTOLOMA, CLITOPILUS. CAP: white or gray tan. GILLS: for *Entoloma* shallow-attached or very short-decurrent; for *Clitopilus* long-decurrent; both white aging spore-color. SPORES: shades of salmon-pink to rose. Found on ground under conifers and hardwoods; all are decomposers of organic debris.

127. ABORTING ENTOLOMA.

Entoloma abortivum. **CAP:** 1½–6″; pale gray or tan; dry; silky. **GILLS:** short-decurrent; close; gray aging salmon-pink. **STEM:** height 1½–5″; gray and velvety above to smooth white at base. **SPORES:** salmon-pink. Found grouped or scattered on ground, at times on rotted wood. The frequently found "aborted" phase (illustrated on left) takes a variety of convoluted rounded shapes. Both phases said to be **EDIBLE.**

128. GRAY ENTOLOMA. *Entoloma lividum.* **CAP:** width 3–7″; gray-tan; sticky in wet weather; margin grooved, downturned. **GILLS:** shallow-attached, subdistant; gray aging salmon. **STEM:** height 1¾–3½″; white, smooth; dry. **SPORES:** bright salmon. Found scattered. **POISONOUS**

129. CROWDED CLITOPILUS.

Clitopilus caespitosus. **CAP:** width 2½–7″; watery white and moist in wet weather, silky-shiny white or pale tan in dry. **GILLS:** short-decurrent; crowded; edges often wavy. **STEM:** height 1½–3½″; silky gray-white. **SPORES:** pale pink. Found clumped, occasionally singly. **DANGEROUS**

130. THE PLUM. *Clitopilus prunulus.* **CAP:** width 2½–5″; white with gray center; dry; powdery; margin aging wavy. **GILLS:** long-decurrent; subdistant. **STEM:** height 1½–4″; dry, smooth; vertically lightly ridged. **SPORES:** pale salmon. Found scattered. **EDIBLE**

LEPTONIA. CAP: center fine-scaled or hairy; aging shallow-depressed. GILLS: shallow-attached. SPORES: pink. Found on ground in wet hardwood and conifer woods, often in mosses. Decomposers of organic debris.

131. BLUE-STEM. *Leptonia asprella.* **CAP:** width ¾–2″; dark brown and margin grooved in wet weather, gray-brown and silky in dry; fuzzy or scaly in center. **Flesh:** white. **GILLS:** subdistant; gray-tinged aging pinkish. **STEM:** height 1½–4″; gray-brown with definite bluish cast; smooth; base white-woolly. Found singly or grouped, often in moss. **DANGEROUS**

132. *Leptonia placida.* **CAP:** width 1½ –2½″; pale gray with dark silky scales, darker in center; margin not grooved. **FLESH:** pink-tinged pale gray. **GILLS:** shallow-attached or with a decurrent tooth; crowded; white aging pink; often wavy-edged. **STEM:** height 1–2½″; dotted lavender or dark blue above to violet or rose below; base white-woolly. Found grouped on rotted hardwoods. **DANGEROUS**

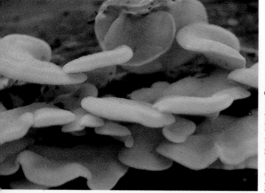

133. SOFT NEST. *Phyllotopsis nidulans.* **CAP:** width ½–4″; bright yellow-orange; plushy; margin down-rolled. **FLESH:** in two layers with upper deeper orange-tan than lower. **GILLS:** fanning from stubby attachment; close to subdistant; orange-yellow. **STEM:** lacking. **SPORES:** pink to flesh-color. Found grouped or shelving on rotting wood which it decomposes. Odor very disagreeable. **NOT RECOMMENDED**

CORTINARIUS.
CAP: convex, bell-shaped, or knobbed; not separable from stem. GILLS: attached then separating; variously colored when young, aging rust-brown; at first covered by cobweblike veil which disappears quickly leaving only colored bands on stem. SPORES: rust-brown or cinnamon. Found on the ground; symbiotic partnerships with trees and shrubs. Because so many of these species are POISONOUS, all species of *Cortinarius* should be avoided. *None* should be eaten!

134. VIOLET CORTINARIUS.
Cortinarius alboviolaceus. **CAP:** width 1½–3½"; pale violet to tan aging silvery; silky-shiny; convex. **FLESH:** pale cap-color. **GILLS:** close; pale violet to gray-purple; edges scalloped. **STEM:** height 2–4"; pale violet at first; white-silky bands near top; bulbous at base. Found scattered under hardwoods, hemlocks, and other conifers. **DANGEROUS**

135. RED GILLS.
Cortinarius semisanguineus. **CAP:** width 1–3"; yellow-brown; silky; dry; convex aging low-knobbed. **FLESH:** pale yellow-tan. **GILLS:** crowded; bright orange to blood-red at first. **STEM:** height 1½–4" (longer when found in moss); yellow; a bit hairy with yellowish bands near top. Found scattered or grouped in low wet places. **DANGEROUS**

136. *Cortinarius evernius.* **CAP:** width 1½–4"; brown-purple in wet weather, silky and paler in dry; margin aging wavy. **FLESH:** about cap-color. **GILLS:** subdistant; cap-color at first; edges remain light. **STEM:** height 5–7' (rarely, 10'); pale at top to deep-violet at base; banded off-white to violet near top. Found grouped or small-clumped under coniifers. **DANGEROUS**

137. *Cortinarius flexipes.* **CAP:** width ½–1¼"; cinnamon with small, shiny, gray-white scales which easily rub off; conical aging bell-shaped. **FLESH:** lavender aging tannish. **GILLS:** close to subdistant; gray-brown with light edge at first. **STEM:** height 1½–2¼"; purplish at top above white bands, white flocked below. Found grouped in low wet places in moss or near pines. **DANGEROUS**

138. DISTANT-GILL CORTI-NARIUS. *Cortinarius distans.* **CAP:** width 1–2½"; red-brown in wet weather, lighter in dry; somewhat scaly; margin often splitting. **FLESH:** brown aging dull yellow. **GILLS:** distant; yellow-brown at first. **STEM:** height 2–4"; brown with light bands; often curved and narrower at base. Found grouped or clumped in open grassy woods. **DANGEROUS**

139. POISON PIE. *Hebeloma crustuliniforme.* **CAP:** width 1¾–3¼"; tan to brownish; margin cream; slimy in wet weather. **FLESH:** white aging tan. **GILLS:** shallow-attached; crowded; white aging light brown; edges fine-wavy; often wet-beaded. **STEM:** height 1½–3½"; white flecked above to smooth below at bulbous base; no veil or ring. **SPORES:** light brown. Found singly or scattered under open-woods trees, with which they form a symbiotic partnership. **POISONOUS**

PHOLIOTA GROUP. *PHOLIOTA, GYMNOPILUS, AGROCYBE, GALERINA, CONOCYBE.* **GILLS:** attached; close or crowded; color aging to that of spores. **RING:** persistent or fragile when present. **SPORES:** some shade of brown. Most are found on wood, of which they are decomposers; a few are found on the ground and reduce other organic debris.

140. EARLY PHOLIOTA. *Pholiota vernalis.* **CAP:** width ½–1½"; satiny gold in dry weather, pale rust with grooved margin in wet; not sticky; central knob depressed with age. **FLESH:** yellow. **GILLS:** attached then separating; close to subdistant; cinnamon. **STEM:** height 1–2"; shiny. **SPORES:** rusty. Found scattered or grouped on dead wood. **EDIBILITY UNKNOWN**

141. WRINKLED PHOLIOTA. *Pholiota rugosa.* **CAP:** width ½–1¼"; yellow-brown in wet weather, yellow-tan and wrinkled surface in dry; dry; conical aging flat with central knob. **FLESH:** cap-color. **GILLS:** pale yellow at first aging light-edged. **STEM:** height 1¼–2"; tan or yellowish, white-mealy above ring, small-scaled below. **SPORES:** cinnamon. Found singly or grouped on rotted wood or moist ground in moist woods. **EDIBILITY UNKNOWN**

142. SCALLOPED PHOLIOTA.
Pholiota albocrenulata. **CAP:** width 1–6″; red-brown to yellow-brown; dark scales aging lighter; very sticky; margin often with ring fragments. **FLESH:** off-white. **GILLS:** attached or notched; pale gray at first; edges white-scalloped. **RING:** fragile. **STEM:** height 1½–7″; off-white to pale yellow; brown-scaled below ring. **SPORES:** cinnamon. Found singly or small clumped on dead or live woods (maple, elm, hemlock). **EDIBILITY UNKNOWN**

143. GOLDEN PHOLIOTA. *Pholiota aurivella.* **CAP:** width 1½–6″; orange with flat, dark scales (may wash off in rain); very sticky; margin often with ring fragments. **FLESH:** pale yellow. **GILLS:** yellow at first. **RING:** fragile. **STEM:** height 1½–5″; yellow becoming spore-stained; not always central. **SPORES:** cinnamon. Found singly or scattered on dead or live hardwoods and conifers. **EDIBLE**

144. FAT PHOLIOTA. *Pholiota adiposa.* **CAP:** width 1½–5″ (or more); yellow with circles of flat, orange-brown scales; very sticky; margin often with ring fragments. **FLESH:** pale yellow. **GILLS:** yellow at first. **RING:** fragile. **STEM:** height 1½–5″; yellow; grainy below ring. **SPORES:** cinnamon. Found singly or clumped on dead or live maple, ash, and other hardwoods. **EDIBLE**

145. SHARP-SCALED PHOLIOTA. *Pholiota squarrosoides.* **CAP:** width 1¼–5″; pale yellow to pale brown; scales brown, pointed, small, denser at center; sticky. **FLESH:** white. **GILLS:** pale yellow or pale olive at first. **RING:** hairy, often disappearing. **STEM:** height 2½–5½″; densely scaly below ring, white and smooth above. **SPORES:** cinnamon. Found densely clumped on dead or live hardwoods. **EDIBLE**

146. SCALY DRY PHOLIOTA.
Pholiota squarrosa. **CAP:** width 1½–6″; yellow to red-brown; scales large and pointed; dry. **Flesh:** pale yellow. **GILLS:** attached to subdecurrent; pale yellow or pale olive at first. **RING:** soft; persistent. **STEM:** height 2–6″; dry; smooth above to densely scaly below ring. **SPORES:** cinnamon. Found densely clumped on dead hardwoods. **EDIBLE**

147. THE DESTROYER. *Pholiota destruens.* **CAP:** width 3–8″; pale yellow
beneath white woolly patches; slightly sticky. **FLESH:** white aging yellow. **GILLS:** notched and separating; white at first. **RING:** very close to gills; loose and fragile. **STEM:** height 1½–9″; white aging spore-color; base bulbous, short "rooting." **SPORES:** cinnamon brown. Found singly or small-clumped on live poplars, birches, and willows. **EDIBLE**

148. BROWN-SPINED LITTLE FLAME. *Pholiota erinaceella.* **CAP:**
width ½–1¼″; red-brown; dense, pointed, tawny-brown scales. **FLESH:** brown with yellow layer under skin. **GILLS:** pale tan at first. **RING:** slight; fragile. **STEM:** height 1–1½″; cap-color; very scaly below ring. **SPORES:** pale cinnamon. Found scattered or grouped on dead wood. **EDIBILITY UNKNOWN**

149. *Pholiota carbonaria.* **CAP:** width
1–2½″; reddish-brown to purple-brown, paler at margin; sticky; scattered tan scales, some hanging on margin. **FLESH:** white. **GILLS:** gray to purple-gray. **STEM:** height 2–3″; brownish-yellow; somewhat silky. **SPORES:** cinnamon brown. Found grouped on charred wood. **NOT RECOMMENDED**

150. RUSTY CLUSTERS. *Gymnopilus luteofolius.* CAP: width 1–4"; dark red to reddish brown, then pinkish red; surface scaly; margin cap color. FLESH: reddish, becoming pale purple. GILLS: attached; yellow becoming yellow orange. RING: cobwebby, pale yellow then more orange. STEM: height 2–4", cap color, streaked with fine hairs. SPORES: orange-rust. Found grouped on rotted wood, especially wood chip mulch. POISONOUS

151. CONIFER GYMNOPILUS. *Gymnopilus sapineus.* CAP: width ¾–3½"; golden to tawny, paler at margin; velvety; often aging cracked. FLESH: pale yellow. GILLS: yellow at first; edges fine-fringed. RING: yellow. STEM: height 2–4½"; yellow bruising brown; silky shiny. SPORES: rusty-yellow. Found singly, scattered, or small-clumped, usually on conifers. EDIBILITY UNKNOWN

152. EARLY AGROCYBE. *Agrocybe praecox.* CAP: width ¾–2½"; whitish tinged tan or cream; smooth or cracked; moist. FLESH: white. GILLS: often separating; white aging light tan. STEM: height 1–3½"; whitish; cobweblike veil, often leaving fragments on cap margin. SPORES: dark brown. Found singly, grouped, or small-clumped on ground in open places. Grows during Spring after heavy rains. *Agrocybe pediades* is very similar. CAP: brown; sticky. Both are EDIBLE.

153. *Galerina autumnalis.* CAP: width 1¼–2½"; dark brown, paling to tan in dry weather; sticky; margin lightly grooved. FLESH: light brown. GILLS: rust-brown. RING: hairy, fragile. STEM: height ¾–3"; white-streaked below ring. SPORES: rusty brown. Found scattered or grouped on rotting wood. DEADLY

154. TENDERHEAD. *Conocybe lactea.* CAP: width 1–1½"; dull white in dry weather, pink-tan in wet; margin lightly grooved; narrowly conical aging bell-shaped. FLESH: whitish. GILLS: almost free; red-brown. RING: lacking. STEM: height 2¼–5"; white, with fine white hairs; enlarging down to white or pale yellow bulb. SPORES: reddish-brown. Found scattered in grass; it wilts in a matter of hours. EDIBILITY UNKNOWN

INOCYBE. CAP: usually some shade of tan or brown; silky, thready; or scaly; most conical aging with low central knob; many split radially to knob. FLESH: white. GILLS: brown when mature. Some have fragile thready veils. SPORES: gray-brown or dingy yellow-brown (never with a red tone). They have symbiotic partnerships with trees and shrubs; found on the ground. All *Inocybe* species are POISONOUS.

155. *Inocybe geophylla.* **CAP:** width ¾– 1½″; white to grayish or lilac; pointed knob; smooth to silky, often aging split. **GILLS:** shallow-attached or notched; close; white aging pale brown. **STEM:** height 1–4″; white to cap-color; finely hairy. Odor unpleasant. Found scattered under hardwoods and conifers. (Also called *Inocybe lilacina.)* **POISONOUS**

156. CONIFER FIBERHEAD. *Inocybe destricta.* **CAP:** width 1–2″; all dark brown or with margin paler; fine-scaly; splitting. **GILLS:** shallow-attached or notched; close; gray-white aging pale gray-brown; edges white-fringed. **STEM:** height 1¼–2½″; pale reddish tan; fuzzy to smooth. Found grouped under pines and hemlocks. **POISONOUS**

157. *Inocybe infelix.* **CAP:** width ½– 1¼″; gray-brown with knob red-brown; thready-scaled. **GILLS:** shallow-attached; close; white aging cinnamon. **STEM:** height 1– 2½″; white or pale violet above to brown below. Found singly or grouped on moist ground. **DEADLY**

158. TORN FIBERHEAD. *Inocybe lacera.* **CAP:** width 1½–2″; fawn to mouse-gray; thready-scaled; ragged around central knob. **GILLS:** shallow-attached; sub-distant; clay-colored. **STEM:** height 1–1½″; brownish with red-brown threads; white-woolly at base. Found scattered under hardwoods. **POISONOUS**

159. VELVET PEG. *Paxillus atroto-mentosus.* **CAP:** width 2½–6″ (or more); rust to black-brown; dry velvety aging smooth; flat or depressed; margin down-rolled. **FLESH:** white. **GILLS:** decurrent; close; forked; tan to brown. **STEM:** height 1½–4″; black-brown, velvety; often off-center. **SPORES:** pale tan. Found singly or clumped on decaying conifers which they decompose. **EDIBLE**

160. FELTY PEG. *Paxillus involutus.* **CAP:** width 2–6″; orange-brown or gray-brown; sticky in wet weather, drying spotted; aging funneled; margin down-rolled and some grooved. **FLESH:** pale yellow bruising brown. **GILLS:** decurrent; olive-yellow bruising brown. **STEM:** height 2–4″; dull yellow-brown or cap-color; smooth. **SPORES:** rust-brown. Found singly or scattered on ground or rotting conifer wood which they decompose. **EDIBILITY UNKNOWN**

CREPIDOTUS They are stemless, or have a short stub from which the gills fan out. SPORES: rusty. They are found on decaying hardwoods and conifer wood which they decompose. All are too thin-fleshed and fragile to be collected for food.

161. LITTLE SHELL. *Crepidotus applanatus.* **CAP:** width ½–2″; white in dry weather, watery pale gray in wet; margin grooved in wet; oval to shell-shaped. **GILLS:** fanning from fuzzy stub; crowded; white aging rusty. Found scattered or grouped. **NOT RECOMMENDED**

162. SOFT SHELL. *Crepidotus mollis.* **CAP:** width ½–2″; yellow-white in dry weather, light brown in wet; gelatinous upper coating is sticky in wet; margin shallow-grooved; smooth. **GILLS:** decurrent; fanning; crowded; white aging rusty. Found in shelving groups. **NOT RECOMMENDED**

AGARICUS. The same genus as the market mushroom, with the wildings having similar profiles. FLESH: white. GILLS: free; pink when very young, quickly graying, then dark spore-color. RING: conspicuous; usually persistent; sometimes double (for example, see number 165). SPORES: dark chocolate brown or deep purple-brown. All are found on the ground and are decomposers of organic debris. Only a few are POISONOUS. Most are EDIBLE.

163. MEADOW MUSHROOM
Agaricus campestris. **CAP:** width 2–4"; white; smooth aging silky-scaly. **FLESH:** thick. **GILLS:** close. **RING:** single; above or about center of stem; some disappear with age. **STEM:** height 2½–4"; white; smooth. **SPORES:** deep chocolate brown. Found scattered in open sunny places. (Very similar to *Agaricus brunnescens,* the commercial mushroom; it is also called *Agaricus bisporus.*) **EDIBLE**

164. BULBED AGARIC. *Agaricus sylvicola.* **CAP:** width 3½–6"; silky white or cream; smooth or with silky fibers. **FLESH:** white bruising yellow; fairly thick. **GILLS:** crowded. **RING:** double; above center of stem. **STEM:** height 4–7½"; cream bruising yellow; base sometimes bulbous. **SPORES:** purple-brown. Found scattered or grouped under hardwoods. **POISONOUS**
Agaricus arvensis is indistinguishable. Found scattered in fields and meadows. It is edible; but because of its similarity to the Bulbed Agaric, it is **NOT RECOMMENDED.**

165. FLAT-TOP AGARIC. *Agaricus placomyces.* **CAP:** width 2½–6"; pale gray-tan dotted with black-brown scales denser over the center; some aging brown. **FLESH:** thin. **GILLS:** crowded. **RING:** double; large; above center of stem. **STEM:** height 3½–6"; white; smooth base bulbous. **SPORES:** black-brown. Found singly or scattered under hardwoods and conifers in forests or cultivated places. **EDIBILITY UNKNOWN**

166. FOREST AGARIC. *Agaricus sylvaticus.* **CAP:** width 1½–5½"; dense, hairy red-brown scales bruising red. **FLESH:** white bruising red-brown. **GILLS:** crowded. **RING:** above center. **STEM:** height 2½–4½"; white-hairy aging pinkish; base often bulbous. **SPORES:** chocolate-brown. Found scattered or grouped, usually under conifers. **EDIBLE**

NAEMATOLOMA, PSATHYRELLA. VEIL:
lacking or fragile; breaking from stem leaving fragments on cap margin and, on some, a faint line or zone on stem. GILLS: attached, then pulling away from stem. SPORES: purple-brown to purple-black. *NAEMATOLOMA.* CAP: fleshy; firm. Found densely clumped on dead wood which it decomposes. *PSATHYRELLA.* CAP: thin; too fragile to supply much food. Found on the ground where it decomposes other organic material.

168. BRICK TOP. *Naematoloma sublateritium.* **CAP:** width 1–3½"; center brick-red with yellow hairs; margin pink-tan and smooth; moist. **FLESH:** tan-white bruising yellowish. **GILLS:** close; white tinged yellow or olive, aging gray-purple; edges white-scalloped. **STEM:** height 2–4"; white and smooth above to brown with flattened hairs below; often yellow-bruised at base. Found clumped on dead hardwoods. **EDIBLE**

169. FRAGILE CAP. *Psathyrella candolleana.* **CAP:** width 1–3½"; off-white, tannish, or yellowish; radially wavy; margin splitting. **FLESH:** white. **GILLS:** close to crowded; white or gray aging purple-brown; edges white-fringed. **STEM:** height 1–2"; shiny white, usually no ring zone. Found grouped or clumped on ground in open woodlands or lawns, rarely on dead wood. **EDIBLE**

167. VELVET PSATHYRELLA. *Psathyrella velutina.* **CAP:** width ½–2"; knobbed center dark brown to tan tinged pink or yellow at margin; dry; velvety; margin splitting. **FLESH:** watery-tan or pale yellow. **GILLS:** almost free; crowded; yellow to tan (often mottled) aging purple-brown; edges white-hairy. **STEM:** height 1–3"; white and hairy above vague veil zone to tan with flattened hairs below. Found singly or grouped on ground in open woods and lawns. **EDIBLE**

COPRINUS. CAP: egg-shaped to cylindrical becoming conical, upturned, with split margins; dissolving into a black liquid. FLESH: white; very thin. GILLS: usually free; aging inky. They are decomposers of wood or other organic debris. For the EDIBLES: pick in the cylindrical stage, before the gills turn dark and cook within one or two hours—all species dissolve completely within twelve hours, sometimes even in a refrigerator. One here is labeled dangerous when alcohol is consumed with it; others *may* be, so be forewarned.

170. GRAY INK-CAP. *Coprinus atramentarius.*
CAP: width 1–3½″; brownish gray with center darker brown and scaly; egg-shaped; margin furrowed, often split. **GILLS:** crowded. **RING:** faint; close to base. **STEM:** height 1½–4½″; shiny white. Found clumped on ground or rotting wood, usually only early spring or late fall. *Do not* consume alcohol before, during, or after eating. Effect is sometimes felt one or two days after eating. **EDIBLE**

171. SHAGGY MANE. *Coprinus comatus.*
CAP: height 2–5″; width 1–2½″, egg shaped or cylindrical; white with red-tan scales aging gray to black and upturned. **GILLS:** notched; crowded. **RING:** thin; movable. **STEM:** height 3–7½″; white; base bulbous. Found scattered or grouped on ground in open places. **EDIBLE**

172. *Coprinus fimetarius.* **CAP:** width 1–2″; gray with brown center; white-flocked aging smooth; furrowed. **GILLS:** close. **STEM:** height 2–5″; white; scaly; base thickens. Found singly or grouped on dung; **EDIBILITY UNKNOWN**

173. GLISTENING INK-CAP.

Coprinus micaceus. **CAP:** width 1–2½″; red-tan to brown in center; furrowed; glistening with tiny granules which quickly disappear. **GILLS:** notched; crowded. **STEM:** height 1½–3″; silky white. Found densely clumped on or near rotting wood. **EDIBLE**

174. JAPANESE UMBRELLA.

Coprinus plicatilis. **CAP:** width ¼–1″; center brown, margin brown aging gray; very fragile; deep-furrowed. **GILLS:** distant; gray; attached to a collar away from stem. **STEM:** height 2–3″; white; smooth; bulbed base. Found scattered on ground, usually in grassy places. **EDIBILITY UNKNOWN**

175. *Coprinus quadrifidus.* **CAP:** height ¾–2′ width; ½–1″, white or pale gray; flaky-scaled aging smooth and fine-furrowed; margin often irregular. **GILLS:** crowded. **RING:** close to white-woolly base. **STEM:** height 2¼–3½″; white; scaly at first, then smooth. Found scattered or clumped on or near decaying wood or hardwoods. **EDIBILITY UNKNOWN**

176. LITTLE GRAY-CAP.

Pseudocoprinus disseminatus. This does not dissolve into inky liquid. **CAP:** width ¼–½″; white aging pale gray with small tan knob; deep-furrowed to knob. **FLESH:** white; very thin. **GILLS:** attached; white aging black. **STEM:** height 1–1½″; white; fine-hairy aging smooth. **SPORES:** black. Found scattered, grouped, or densely clumped near decaying wood or compost . **EDIBILITY UNKNOWN**

177. MOWER'S MUSHROOM.

Panaeolus foenisecii. **CAP:** ½–1¼″; gray-brown to burgundy-brown in wet weather, tan with metallic luster in dry; appearing zoned in drying process. **FLESH:** pale tan, thin. **GILLS:** attached, often aging notched; sub-distant; edges white-fringed. **STEM:** height 2–4″; pale tan; fine-hairy at top to smooth below. **SPORES:** dark purple-brown. Found scattered or dense-clumped in grassy places. **POISONOUS**

178. LITTLE NAIL. *Chroogomphus*

vinicolor. **CAP:** width ½–1″; dark wine-red to rusty or copper with margin paler; conical with pointed knob; sticky. **FLESH:** pink. **GILLS:** decurrent; distant; olive-brown or smoky, often dark-speckled. **STEM:** height 1½–2″; sticky; cap-color; silky. **SPORES:** dark smoky-brown to black. Found singly or grouped under pine and hemlock in wet forests, forming a symbiotic partnership with trees. **EDIBILITY UNKNOWN**

179. SHINY NAIL. *Chroogomphus*

rutilus. **CAP:** width 1–5½″; rusty; small-knobbed; sticky. **FLESH:** pink under skin to yellow near stem. **GILLS:** decurrent; distant; tan to cinnamon. **STEM:** height 2–7″; dry to moist; tan with reddish cast on thready central veil remains. **SPORES:** smoky-gray to black. Found singly or grouped under conifers, forming a symbiotic partnership. **EDIBLE**

BOLETES. *GYRODON, STROBILOMYCES, SUILLUS, BOLETUS, LECCINUM, GYROPORUS, TYLOPILUS.* CAP and STEM: fleshy; from above look like gilled mushrooms. Underside of cap is conspicuously different: a surface with PORES, or pin-prick holes. PORE SURFACE: color always ages to that of the spores. For species identification, in addition to spore and pore surface color, note color change—if any—of flesh and tubes when broken or bruised. Found on the ground, rising from root system of the woody plants with which they form symbiotic partnerships.

180. VEINED BOLETE. *Gyrodon merulioides.*
CAP: width 2–5″; yellow-brown to red-brown; dry; felty. **TUBES:** decurrent; veiny and yellow. **PORE SURFACE:** yellow. **FLESH:** yellow; usually unchanging but at times slowly bruising blue-green. **STEM:** height ¾–1½″; cap-color, darker at base; somewhat off-center. **SPORES:** olive-brown. Found scattered on moist ground, usually under ash trees. **EDIBLE**

181. OLD MAN OF THE WOODS. *Strobilomyces floccopus.*
CAP: width 1½–6″; gray woolly tufts on dark brown to black; margin with gray veil fragments. **TUBES:** usually attached. **PORE SURFACE:** gray. **FLESH:** (cap and stem): pale gray-tan slowly bruising reddish then black. **STEM:** height 2–5″; pale and smooth above ring, cap-texture and cap-color below. **SPORES:** black. Found singly or scattered under hardwoods—often oak—and conifers. **EDIBLE**

182. AMERICAN BOLETE. *Suillus americanus.*
CAP: width 1–4¼″; yellow with tan to cinnamon patches; margin with veil fragments; sticky. **TUBES:** attached or decurrent. **PORE SURFACE:** mustard yellow at first. **FLESH:** yellow bruising brown. **RING:** lacking. **STEM:** height 1–3½″ yellow dotted brown, bruising brown; dry. **SPORES:** dull cinnamon. Found singly, scattered, or clumped under white pine. **EDIBLE**

183. GRANULAR BOLETE. *Suillus granulatus.*
CAP: width 2–5″; medium red-brown or yellow with red-brown center (some aging solid yellow); sticky. **TUBES:** attached or depressed aging short-decurrent. **PORE SURFACE:** yellow. **FLESH:** (cap and stem): pale lemon-yellow. **STEM:** height 1½–4″; bright yellow dotted orange. **SPORES:** light olive-brown. Found grouped or clumped under pines. *Suillus brevipes* is very similar. **STEM:** height up to 1″, dots are lacking. Both are **EDIBLE.**

184. SLIPPERY JACK. *Suillus luteus.* **CAP:** width 2–4½"; dark red-brown; slimy to sticky. **TUBES:** attached to subdecurrent. **PORE SURFACE:** yellow aging dark-dotted. **FLESH:** white or pale yellow; unchanging. **RING:** near top. **STEM:** height 1½–3"; cap-color; sticky. **SPORES:** cinnamon. Found scattered or grouped under conifers. **EDIBLE**

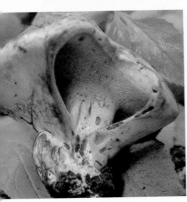

185. LEATHER COLLAR. *Suillus sphaerosporus.* **CAP:** width 2–6" (or more); yellow-tan aging dark yellow-brown and spotted; sticky in wet weather. **TUBES:** attached or decurrent. **PORE SURFACE:** yellow bruising and aging brown. **FLESH:** pale yellow to white bruising red-brown. **RING:** leathery-tough; almost at base. **STEM:** height 1½–4". **SPORES:** olive-yellow. Found singly or grouped under hardwoods, particularly oak. **NOT RECOMMENDED**

186. MOCK OYSTER. *Suillus cavipes.* **CAP:** width 1–4"; dull yellow to red-brown; tawny dense-hairy; margin with whitish veil fragments; dry, moist in wet weather. **TUBES:** decurrent. **PORE SURFACE:** yellow at first. **FLESH:** white aging yellowish; unchanging. **RING:** fragile. **STEM:** height 1½–3½"; yellow above to cap-color below ring; dry. **SPORES:** olive-brown. Found grouped or clumped under tamaracks. **EDIBLE**

187. PAINTED LADY. *Suillus pictus.* **CAP:** width 1–4½″; red with gray thready hairs; margin with whitish veil fragments; dry, a bit sticky in wet weather. **TUBES:** attached to decurrent. **PORE SURFACE:** bright yellow bruising red-brown. **FLESH:** yellow bruising pink-gray to reddish. **STEM:** height 1½–4″; yellow above to whitish and hairy below ring. **SPORES:** olive-brown. Found scattered or grouped under white pine. **EDIBLE**

188. LURID BOLETE. *Boletus luridus.* **CAP:** width 2–5″; mixture of yellow, olive, red, and brown bruising green-blue; felty in dry weather, sticky in wet. **TUBES:** deeply depressed to free. **PORE SURFACE:** dark red bruising green-blue. **FLESH:** whitish bruising blue. **STEM:** height 2–6″; yellow flushed orange and red; flesh yellow bruising blue. **SPORES:** olive to olive-brown. Found singly or grouped under hardwoods and conifers. **POISONOUS**

189. PAINTED BOLETE. *Boletus chromapes.* **CAP:** width 2–4½″; pink to pale pink; sticky or dry. **TUBES:** depressed. **PORE SURFACE:** pink aging pale yellow-brown. **FLESH:** white, pink under skin. **STEM:** height 3–5½″; bent; shades of pink and brownish yellow; base yellow, upper part with pink dots. **SPORES:** pinkish-brown. Found scattered under hardwoods and conifers. **EDIBLE**

190. ORANGE BOLETE. *Leccinum aurantiacum.* **CAP:** width 2-6″; bright or dull rust-orange; dry velvety. **TUBES:** depressed to almost free. **PORE SURFACE:** olive-tan bruising brown. **FLESH:** (cap and stem): white slowly bruising purplish then gray. **STEM:** height 4-6½″; whitish to pale tan with brown or black speckles. **SPORES:** yellow-brown. Found singly or scattered under pines and aspens. **EDIBLE**

191. ROUGH-STEM BOLETE. *Leccinum scabrum.* **CAP:** width 1½-4″; gray-brown or yellow-brown aging olive-brown; smooth; sticky in wet weather. **TUBES:** deeply depressed. **PORE SURFACE:** pink-tan at first. **FLESH:** (cap and stem): white; unchanging or slowly bruising pink-tan. **STEM:** height 3-5½″; whitish with dark brown to black speckles. **SPORES:** yellow-brown. Found scattered or grouped, usually under birch. *Leccinum insigne* is similar. **FLESH:** stains red to purple or gray. Both are **EDIBLE.**

192. BLUE STAINER. *Gyroporus cyanescens.* **CAP:** width 1½-5″; pale straw color; pitted or wrinkled; dry. **TUBES:** deeply depressed. **PORE SURFACE:** white to cream aging olive-yellow. **FLESH:** pale cream. **STEM:** height 1½-4″; cap-color. **SPORES:** pale yellow. Pore surface, flesh, and stem all instantly bruise indigo. Found singly, grouped, or clumped under hardwoods. **EDIBLE**

193. BITTER BOLETE. *Tylopilus felleus.* **CAP:** width 2–6″ (rarely to 12″); tan aging brownish; dry felty; a bit sticky in wet weather. **TUBES:** decurrent aging depressed. **PORE SURFACE:** whitish aging deep pink, bruising brownish. **FLESH:** white; unchanging or bruising pinkish. **STEM:** height 1½–5″; brown-netted tan. **SPORES:** deep pink. Found singly or scattered on hemlock debris or under conifers and hardwoods. **NOT RECOMMENDED**

POLYPORES. These fungi are like the Boletes but are usually hard or tough rather than fragile like a mushroom. They are often shelved brackets or conks, protruding from rotted wood or a living tree. PORES: may be very small or up to ⅛″ in diameter. STEM; central, off-center, lateral, or lacking. Most cause decay of wood. Few are EDIBLE.

194. SWEET TRAMETES. *Trametes suaveolens.* **BODY:** width 2–6½″; white, gray or yellow-brown in age; not zoned; velvety to smooth; soft-corky aging tough. **PORE SURFACE:** white aging dark. **FLESH:** white; depth to ⅜″; anise-scented when fresh. Found scattered or shelved on dead or dying willow, rarely on birch and poplar. **NOT RECOMMENDED**

195. BIRCH CONK. *Piptoporus betulinus.* **BODY:** width 1¼–10″; (oval-flat to round, hanging down or with a lateral stem.); tan thin skin may split leaving white cracks; smooth; margin thick, inrolled, extending over edge of pore surface; spongy aging corky. **PORE SURFACE:** white aging tan. **FLESH:** white; depth to 1¼″. Found scattered on live or dead birch. **NOT RECOMMENDED**

196. *Tyromyces albellus.* **BODY:** width ½–5″; white aging grayish or yellowish; fine-velvety to smooth; watery-soft aging rigid. **PORE SURFACE:** white or yellowish. **FLESH:** white; depth to 1″. Found scattered on dead hardwood, rarely conifers. *Tyromyces spraguei* is similar. **MARGIN:** tan staining green on bruising. Found especially on oaks. Both are **NOT RECOMMENDED.**

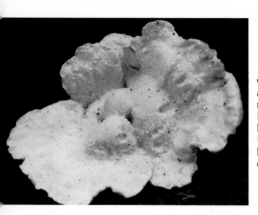

197. *Climacodon borealis.* **BODY:** width 1½–6′ or clumped to 15″ across; white aging yellowish and rough; when clumped may have a stemlike central base; tough aging hard. **PORE SURFACE:** uneven aging maze-like or toothed. **FLESH:** white; very thin or to ¾″ deep. Found singly or clumped on dead or live conifers, rarely on hardwood. **NOT REC-OMMENDED**

198. THE SPONGE. *Spongipellis unicolor.* **BODY:** width 1½–14″; white aging gray or yellowish; hairy; margin thick, rounded; spongy aging corky. **PORE SUR-FACE:** toothed; white aging yellowish or tan. **FLESH:** white; depth to 1¼″; Found singly or scattered on live hardwood. **NOT RECOM-MENDED**

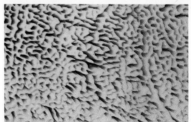

199. TURKEY TAIL. *Coriolus versicolor.* **BODY:** width ¾–3′ (or more), often clumped to 10′; multicolor zoned; fine-velvety to smooth; margin thin, leathery aging rigid. **PORE SURFACE:** white or yellowish aging brownish. **FLESH:** white; very thin. Found in crowded shelves or rosetted clumps on dead or injured hardwood, rarely on conifers. **NOT RECOMMENDED**

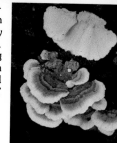

200. *Oxyporus populinus.* **BODY:** width 1¼–7′; white to grayish aging tan; silky-hairy; margin may be short-hairy; often moss-covered; watery or corky aging firm. **PORE SURFACE:** white to cream-yellow. **FLESH:** white or pale tan; depth to ⅜″. Found in shelving groups on live maples, rarely on other hardwoods. **NOT RECOMMENDED**

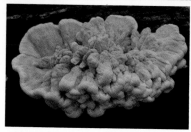

201. SULPHUR SHELF. *Laetiporus sulphureus.* **BODY:** width 2¾–12½″, clusters to 25″ across; zoned bright orange to yellow aging tannish; fleshy-watery aging brittle hard. **PORE SURFACE:** yellow. **FLESH:** white, pale yellow or pale salmon; depth to ¾″. Found in crowded shelves on trunks or rosettes on hardwood roots, especially oak, rarely on conifers. *Laetiporus semialbinus* is similar. **PORE SURFACE:** white. Both are **EDIBLE.**

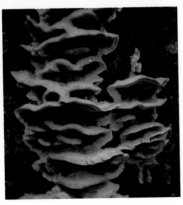

202. SCORCHED BRACKET.
Bjerkandera adusta. **BODY:** width 1¼–4½″; white, pale gray, tan, or red-blotched; silky or smooth; corky-tough aging hard. **PORE SURFACE:** gray or gray-black bruising blackish. **FLESH:** white; depth to ½″. Found turned out or shelved on dead hardwood, especially poplar, rarely on conifers. *Bjerkandera fumosa* is very similar but somewhat thicker. Both are **NOT RECOMMENDED**

203. *Polyporus conchifer.* **BODY:** width ½–2″; cup white or whitish; ridged (at first not developed); saucer persistent, flat on host, white or light brown; leathery aging brittle. **PORE SURFACE:** white or whitish. **FLESH:** white; very thin. Found scattered on dead hardwood, particularly elm. **NOT RECOMMENDED**

204. *Gloeoporus dichrous.* **BODY:** width ½–3¼″; whitish; hairy or velvety; leathery aging rigid. **PORE SURFACE:** flesh-color, red-purple, or purple-black; waxy. **FLESH:** white; very thin. Found shelved on dead hardwood, rarely conifers. **NOT RECOMMENDED**

205. PARCHMENT BRACKET.
Hirschioporus pargamenus (on hardwood); *Hirschioporus abietina* (on conifers). **BODY:** width ½–3″; zoned white to dark or light tan; margin lavender, ruffled; velvety; flexible. **PORE SURFACE:** white with lavender margin. **FLESH:** white; very thin. Found in crowded shelves on dead wood, sometimes merely as a lavender to nearly purple pore layer on host. **NOT RECOMMENDED**

206. ORANGE SHELF. *Pycnoporus cinnabarinus.* **BODY:** width ¾–5″; bright rusty-orange; fuzzy aging smooth and furrowed; leathery-tough aging hard; **PORE SURFACE:** brilliant rusty-orange. **FLESH:** red-orange; depth to ½″. Found scattered or shelved on dead hardwood, rarely on conifers. **NOT RECOMMENDED**

Similar to the Orange Shelf is

207. *Pycnoporus sanguineus.* **BODY:** ¾–3″; bright red-orange; fine-velvety to smooth; margin very thin; pliable aging rigid. **PORE SURFACE:** brilliant orange-red. **FLESH:** orange red or red; very thin. Found singly, rosetted, or shelved on dead hardwood. This fungus is more common in the South. **NOT RECOMMENDED**

208. ARTIST'S PALETTE. *Ganoderma applanatum.* **BODY:** width 2¼–20″; brown, grayish, or black-gray becoming brown-spore dusted; margin tan when young; hard-crusted; smooth; corky aging hard. **PORE SURFACE:** whitish bruising or marking dark brown. **FLESH:** brown; depth to 2″. Found scattered or shelved on dead or living hardwood, rarely on conifers. **NOT RECOMMENDED**

209. *Inonotus obliquus.* **BODY:** up to 12 x 6′; black; irregular mass; deeply cracked throughout; hard and brittle. **FLESH:** orange-brown. This is the sterile conk of a rarely encountered pore fungus. Almost entirely restricted to birch. **NOT RECOMMENDED**

210. VELVET TOP. *Phaeolus schweinitzii.* **BODY:** width 2–10″; zoned tan to orange or rust; velvety or almost woolly; may have central stem to 2½″, color of top; watery-spongy aging hard and brittle. **PORE SURFACE:** yellowish to gray-yellow or olive aging and bruising brown. **FLESH:** yellow-brown to red-brown; depth to 1¼″. Found scattered or shelved low on trunks or buried roots of conifers, rarely on hardwood. **NOT RECOMMENDED**

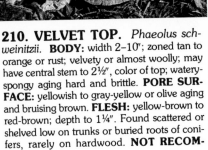

211. GOLDEN BRACKET. *Phellinus gilvus.* **BODY:** width 1–5″ (or more); reddish-brown aging yellow-brown or dark rust; velvety aging rough; leathery-corky aging rigid. **PORE SURFACE:** red-brown aging gray-brown. **FLESH:** yellow-brown; depth to ⅜″. Found shelved on dead hardwood, rarely on conifers. **NOT RECOMMENDED**

212. TINDERWOOD. *Fomes fomentarius.* **BODY:** width 2½–8′; latest annual layer tan and velvety; aging gray or gray-black and crusty; hard corky. **PORE SURFACE:** gray to brown. **FLESH:** light or dark brown; each year's depth to 1″. Found scattered on upright dead or live hardwood. **NOT RECOMMENDED**

213. RED BELT. *Fomitopsis pinicola.* **BODY:** width 2½–15″; red, brown, or blackish aging gray to black and crusted; flat hoof-shaped; new year's margin thick, tan, often with clear to yellow droplets on pore surface or margin; hard-corky from the beginning. **PORE SURFACE:** white, tan, or light yellow bruising yellow or lavender. **FLESH:** pale to dark tan bruising pinkish; depth to ⅝″ yearly. Found scattered on dead hardwood and conifers. **NOT RECOMMENDED**

214. THE CLINKER. *Phellinus tremulae.* **BODY:** width 2–8″; annual layer brown and velvety; aging gray to black and smooth and cracked; hoof-shaped; woody-hard from beginning. **PORE SURFACE:** gray-brown to brown. **FLESH:** brown; yearly depth to ⅜″. Found scattered on live aspen. (Also called *Phellinus Igniarius* in many books.) **NOT RECOMMENDED**

215. NEST BRACKET. *Hapalopilus nidulans.* **BODY:** width ¾–3½″; pale yellow-brown or pinkish-brown aging and bruising reddish or purplish; velvety to smooth; hoof-shaped; margin may be yellow; watery-soft aging rigid. **PORE SURFACE:** yellow or red-brown. **FLESH:** color of top; depth ¾–2″. Found singly or scattered on dead hardwood, rarely on conifers. **NOT RECOMMENDED**

216. LACQUER TOP. *Ganoderma tsugae* (on conifers); *Ganoderma lucidum* (on hardwoods). **BODY:** width 2¼–14″; orange-brown with gold margin aging dark mahogany overall and radially wrinkled; crusty; shining except when dusted with brown spores; corky aging hard. **PORE SURFACE:** pale to dark tan. **FLESH:** white or pale tan; depth to 1″. **STEM:** length to 5″; lateral; color of top; crusted when present. Found singly or scattered on dead wood or buried roots. **NOT RECOMMENDED**

217. SCALY POLYPORE. *Polyporus squamosus.* **BODY:** width 2–12″; brown-scaly or tan; convex to centrally depressed; soft-corky. **PORE SURFACE:** white or yellowish; pores large. **FLESH:** white; depth to 1½″. **STEM:** length ¼–2″; lateral or central. Found singly or shelving on live hardwood, rarely on dead. **NOT RECOMMENDED**

218. HONEYCOMB. *Favolus alveolaris.* **BODY:** width ½–4″; orange to brick-red; threaded or with small scales; aging cream and smooth; fleshy-tough aging hard. **PORE SURFACE:** decurrent; white aging yellowish; pores large. **FLESH:** white; very thin. **STEM:** short stub; lateral. Found scattered on dead hardwood branches. **NOT RECOMMENDED**

219. HEN OF THE WOODS. *Grifola frondosa.* **BODY:** height 10–20″; crowded, overlapping short-stemmed fans laterally attached to stem. **FAN:** width 1–3½″; zoned brown or gray; velvety; pliable. **PORE SURFACE:** decurrent; white. **FLESH:** white; very thin. **STEM:** thick; central; Found on ground on buried roots or stumps of hardwood, rarely on conifers. **EDIBLE**

220. BIG ROSETTE. *Grifola gigantea.* **BODY:** width 6–15″; overlapping circular shells attached to short thick central stem. **SHELL:** diameter 2½–6″; zoned tan to smoky brown; velvety; radially furrowed; tough-pliable. **PORE SURFACE:** white bruising and aging blackish. **FLESH:** white; thin. Found on ground in overlapping rosettes on buried roots of hardwood. **NOT RECOMMENDED**

221. LITTLE BUTTON. *Polyporus arcularius.* **CAP:** width ½–3″; gold-brown to dark brown; small-scaled; margin thready; tough aging rigid. **PORE SURFACE:** yellowish to white. **FLESH:** white; thin. **STEM:** height ¾–2½″; brown; central. Found scattered or grouped on dead hardwood. **NOT RECOMMENDED**

222. SOOTY POLYPORE. *Polyporus brumalis.* **CAP:** width 1–2½″ (or more); light to dark brown or blackish; dense-hairy aging velvety or smooth; margin often hairy; leathery aging rigid. **PORE SURFACE:** decurrent; off-white. **FLESH:** white, thin. **STEM:** height 1–2½″; gray or brown; central or off-center. Found scattered on dead hardwood (rarely conifers). **NOT RECOMMENDED**

223. BLACK FOOT. *Polyporus elegans.* **CAP:** width ¾–3″; tan; leathery aging brittle hard. **PORE SURFACE:** decurrent; gray or tan. **FLESH:** whitish; very thin. **STEM:** height ½–3″; tan above to black at base; central or lateral. Found scattered on dead hardwood branches and twigs, rarely on conifers. **NOT RECOMMENDED**

224. BLACK STEM. *Polyporus picipes.* **CAP:** width 1½–8″; hazel to chestnut brown aging black; smooth; usually depressed over stem, leathery aging rigid. **PORE SURFACE:** decurrent; white to tan. **FLESH:** white; thin. **STEM:** height ½–2½″; all black or lower half black; central or lateral. Found scattered on hardwood logs and stumps, rarely on conifers. **NOT RECOMMENDED**

225. ROOTED POLYPORE. *Polyporus radicatus.* **CAP:** width 1½–10″; yellow or reddish-brown to dark gray-brown; velvety or scaly aging centrally smooth; tough-fleshy aging rigid; often centrally depressed. **PORE SURFACE:** decurrent; white or yellowish. **FLESH:** white; depth to ⅜″. **STEM:** height 2½–5″ (or more); scaly; central; long black root in soil. Found on ground on buried roots of hardwoods. **NOT RECOMMENDED**

226. GROUND FUNNEL. *Coltricia perennis.* **CAP:** ⅜–3″; zoned gray-brown to red-brown; velvety; funneled; leathery aging rigid. **PORE SURFACE:** decurrent; yellow-brown to red-brown or gray. **FLESH:** brown; very thin. **STEM:** height ⅜–3″; brown; velvety; central. Found scattered or grouped on open ground, rarely on wood. *Coltricia cinnamomea* is similar. **CAP:** silky; shining. Both are **NOT RECOMMENDED.**

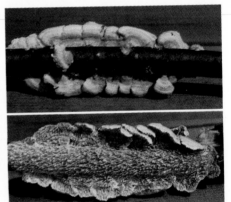

227. *Antrodia mollis.* **BODY:** thin patches flat on host or with edges turned up or out; zoned gray-brown to blackish; velvety aging smooth; leathery aging firm. **PORE SURFACE:** gray to brown; pores large and toothy. **FLESH:** light brown with black line next to skin; very thin. Found on wood of dead hardwood. **NOT RECOMMENDED**

228. *Irpex lacteus.* **BODY:** dense patches of pore surface lying flat on host with velvety edges turned back. **PORE SURFACE:** white or yellowish; aging mazelike or toothed. **FLESH:** white; very thin. Found on dead hardwood branches or twigs. **NOT RECOMMENDED**

229. BROWN CRUST. *Phellinus punctatus.* **BODY:** large perennial patches, depth to 1¼″, flat on host; gray-brown or red-brown; margin yellow-brown aging dark red-brown; receding annually and giving rest of crust a humped look. **FLESH:** dark red-brown; thin; firm. Found on underside of logs, or small branches of dead hardwood, rarely on conifers. **NOT RECOMMENDED**

230. LITTLE BIRCH SHELF. *Lenzites betulina.* **BODY:** width ¾–5″; zoned gray, yellow, and orange aging grayish; velvety; pliable aging firm. **UNDERSURFACE:** gill-like; white or off-white. **FLESH:** white; thin. **STEM:** lacking. Found scattered or shelved on dead hardwood, rarely on conifers. **NOT RECOMMENDED**

231. CHOCOLATE SHELF. *Gloeophyllum sepiarium.* (on conifers); *Gloeophyllum trabeum* (on hardwood). **BODY:** width ¾–4″; zoned white, orange, and brown; velvety; leathery aging rigid. **UNDERSURFACE:** gill-like, mazelike, or pored; brown. **FLESH:** yellow-brown or rusty; thin. **STEM:** lacking. Found scattered or shelved on dead wood, also on structures and buildings. **NOT RECOMMENDED**

232. CURRYCOMB. *Daedalia confragosa.* **BODY:** width 1¼–6″; zoned gray to smoky-brown aging blackish; fine velvety or smooth; leathery aging rigid. **UNDERSURFACE:** mazelike to pored; white or tan bruising pinkish. **FLESH:** whitish or tan; depth to ⅜″. **STEM:** lacking. Found scattered or shelved on dead or live hardwood. **NOT RECOMMENDED**

233. *Cerrena unicolor.* **BODY:** width ¾–3¼"; zoned white, gray, yellowish, and brown, often green-tinted over surface from algal growth on surface; woolly to hairy; leathery aging firm. **UNDERSURFACE:** mazelike (may age toothed); white to gray. **FLESH:** white or whitish; very thin. **STEM:** lacking. Found shelved on dead hardwood, rarely on conifers. **NOT RECOMMENDED**

THE THELEPHORES

THE THELEPHORES. This group of mushroom relatives is characterized by spores being borne on a SMOOTH or slightly roughened surface. No gills, pores, or teeth are formed on the lower surface of the body, which is often flattened on the host, on turned out caps, or on caps with a lateral stem. Most are thin bodied, somewhat leathery, and grow on wood. All are **NOT RECOMMENDED.**

234. GRAY-CUP. *Aleurodiscus oakesii.* **BODY:** width to ⅜"; gray to pale gray; mealy flat cups with margins curled up; shrinking in dry weather, expanding in wet. **SPORE SURFACE:** pink to creamy pink. Found scattered or in crowded groups on bark of hardwood, particularly white oak. **NOT RECOMMENDED**

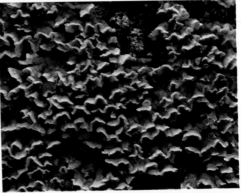

235. CROWDED STEREUM. *Stereum complicatum.* **BODY:** densely overlapping thin lobes to ⅜" across; zoned brown to gold-tan; in dry weather brittle and margin curled, pliable and expanded again in wet. **SPORE SURFACE:** orange. Found on dead twigs and stumps of hardwood. This is the most common *Stereum* in North America. **NOT RECOMMENDED**

236. WOOD KNOBS. *Xylobolus frustulatus.* **BODY:** crowded groups of tiny grooved woody knobs; upper side black, crusty; whitish to tan below. Found on dead oak, often on the underside of fallen logs. **NOT RECOMMENDED**

237. STEREUM OSTREA.

BODY: lies flat on log or fans up to 2' wide; rubbery to leathery, upperside with gray to green hairs in rings; lower surface yellow-brown to reddish-brown; smooth. Found on hardwood logs, especially oak. **NOT RECOMMENDED**

238. THELEPHORA TERRESTRIS.

BODY: arises as fan or funnel, dark gray to black on top; leathery; pale gray to gray-brown on bottom. Found on ground or surrounding bases of plants at soil line in conifer forests. **NOT RECOMMENDED**

239. RED BUBBLES. *Peniophora rufa.*

BODY: crowded groups of tiny grooved woody knobs about ⅛" across; upperside red, whitish to tan below. Found on dead alder, on the underside of branches. **NOT RECOMMENDED**

JELLY FUNGI. Usually most conspicuous in wet or damp weather. They are decomposers of the wood on which most are found or of other organic debris. None is considered dangerous, but all are too small, tasteless, or ill-smelling to collect to eat.

240. TOOTHED JELLY. *Pseudo-hydnum gelatinosum.* **CAP:** width 1¼– 2¼″; translucent white aging brownish; tough-gelatinous with blunt-spined undersurface. **STEM:** lateral; short. Found singly to scattered on rotted conifer wood, often among moss. **NOT RECOMMENDED**

241. PALE WITCH'S BUTTER. *Tremella lutescens.* **BODY:** width ⅜–1¼″; sulphur to pale yellow jellylike translucent lobes; tough-gelatinous drying brittle and reviving after later rains. Found singly or scattered on dead hardwood twigs and branches. **NOT RECOMMENDED**

242. GOLDEN WITCH'S BUT-TER. *Tremella mesenterica.* **BODY:** width ¾–4″; orange to golden translucent jellylike lobes or globules; tough-gelatinous drying brittle and reviving after later rains. Found singly or scattered on dead hardwood. **NOT RECOMMENDED**

243. LEAFY JELLY. *Tremella foliacea.* **BODY:** height to 1¾"; flesh-color to cinnamon aging black-brown and slimy; crowded clusters of thin leaflike folds spreading to 6' (or more) across; firm-gelatinous aging mushy. Found on dead hardwood and conifers. **NOT RECOMMENDED**

244. WHITE TREMELLA. *Tremella fuciformis.* **BODY:** width to 2'; translucent white; forked gelatinous to ends; slimy. Found on hardwood branches. **NOT RECOMMENDED**

245. HOLLOW-LOBED TREMELLA. *Tremella reticulata.* **BODY:** height 1¼–4½"; white aging brown; coral- or fingerlike; gelatinous to slimy; erect, elastic, hollow lobes usually fused. Found in large rosettes on ground or very rotted wood. **NOT RECOMMENDED**

246. WHITE BLANKET. *Tremella cancrescens.* **BODY:** white aging grayish; "cotton batting" coating on ground becoming tough gelatinous on debris, or bases of living plants; may form small erect branches. Found in masses to 10' (or more). **NOT RECOMMENDED**

247. BLACK JELLY. *Exidia glandulosa.* **BODY:** to ¾″ fused to 8′ across; brown-black irregular gelatinous globules drying to black paper-thin chips. Found scattered or clustered on dead hardwood. **NOT RECOMMENDED**

248. SHARP ANTLERS. *Calocera cornea.* **BODY:** height to ¾″; yellow drying red-brown; upright stalks, simple or branched, with pointed tips; firm-gelatinous drying brittle; shallow "rooted." Found grouped or clustered on dead hardwood or bark, rarely on conifer. **NOT RECOMMENDED**

249. FLAT-STEM JELLY. *Tremellodendron pallidum.* **BODY:** height to 1¾″; width to 6′; cream-white aging tan; dry; erect flattened branching stalks with irregularly cut-off tops, fused to a single base; tough-waxy drying brittle. Found rosetted on ground under hardwood and conifers. **NOT RECOMMENDED**

250. BLUNT ANTLERS. *Calocera viscosa.* **BODY:** height 1¼-4″; golden to orange-yellow, white at base; upright branching sticky stalks with blunt tips; tough gelatinous drying brittle; deep "rooted." Found grouped on dead conifer wood. **NOT RECOMMENDED**

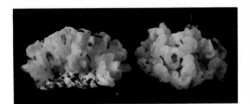

251. FAIRY BUTTER. *Dacrymyces palmatus.* **BODY:** width to 2½"; bright orange to orange-red with white base; brainlike folded; gelatinous aging slimy. Found clustered on dead conifers. *Dacrymyces capitata* is very similar but usually found on hardwood. Both are **NOT RECOMMENDED**

252. *Dacrymyces stillatus.* **BODY:** width to ¼"; lemon to amber drying red-brown; tough-gelatinous flattened top-shape aging to short-stemmed cups. Found scattered or grouped on dead wood. (Also called *Dacrymyces delequescens.*) **NOT RECOMMENDED**

TOOTHED FUNGI

TOOTHED FUNGI. On the underside, all have soft, fleshy, comblike teeth or spines on which their spores are held to maturity. SPORES: usually white. Those found on the ground form symbiotic partnerships with trees; those on dead wood are decomposers; and one uses only pine cones for sustenance.

253. HEDGEHOG. *Dentinum repandum.* **CAP:** width ¾–4"; peach or yellow-tan; smooth; **FLESH:** pale yellow; **TEETH:** decurrent, cream. **STEM:** height ¾–3¼"; white, smooth; may be off-center. Found singly or grouped under hardwoods and conifers. **EDIBLE**

254. SHINGLE CAP. *Hydnum imbricatum.* **CAP:** width 3–8' (sometimes to 15"); tan with large, raised brown scales; **FLESH:** white to tan, tough; **TEETH:** decurrent; brown, coarse. **STEM:** height 2½–4"; tan; smooth; base enlarged. **SPORES:** brown. Found singly or scattered under hardwoods and conifers. **EDIBLE**

255. STEMMED EAR. *Auriscalpium vulgare.* **CAP:** width to 1¾"; brown to almost black; dense-hairy; heart-shape; **FLESH:** tan; **TEETH:** needlelike, white, later brownish; shriveling in dry weather, reviving in wet. **STEM:** height to 3¼"; dark brown, hairy; attached to side of cap. Found singly or scattered on cones of conifers. **NOT RECOMMENDED**

256. LARGE WHITE CORAL. *Hericium coralloides.* **BODY:** width 2–12"; white aging tan; **TEETH:** *at ends of* branches extending from central stalk. Found singly or scattered on dead wood of hardwood. **EDIBLE**

257. BEAR'S HEAD. *Hericium ramosum.* **BODY:** width 2–11"; white aging tan; **TEETH:** interlacing; on *underside* of branches extending from central stalk. Found singly or scattered on dead hardwood. **EDIBLE**

106

258. MEDUSA'S HEAD. *Hericium erinaceus.* **BODY:** width 2–12″; white aging tan; **TEETH:** unbranched crowded; hanging from central mass. Found singly growing from wounds on live hardwoods. **EDIBLE**

259. TOOTHED BRACKET. *Climacodon septentrionale.* **BODY:** width 6–12″; buff aging yellow-brown; hairy. **FLESH:** to 1½″ thick, white, tough; **TEETH:** thin, whitish, to ¾″ long. **STEM:** lacking. Found in large overlapping shelves on live hardwood, particularly maple. **NOT RECOMMENDED**

260. BLACK VELVET. *Phellodon niger.* **CAP:** 2–3′ width; pale gray to dark brownish-gray at center; flattened depressed; velvety. **FLESH:** two-layered, layer of cap-colored soft flesh over black hard flesh; **TEETH:** light gray, black when bruised. **STEM:** height 1–2′; central, swollen at base; felty. Found on ground under pines and spruce. **NOT RECOMMENDED**

CLUB FUNGI

CLUB FUNGI. These vary from single "clubs" to colonies to crowded branching stalks. They are flexible to brittle (none hard or sticky). All carry their spores on surfaces above the base. Most form symbiotic partnerships with the trees under or on which they are found. They are difficult to clean, but many are **EDIBLE.**

261. INDIAN CLUB. *Clavariadelphus pistillaris.* **BODY:** height 2½–8′; yellowish, tan, or light red-brown; vertically wrinkled; top rounded tapering to lighter base. **FLESH:** white. **SPORES:** white. Found singly, scattered, or grouped under hardwood and conifers. Has a bitter-peppery flavor, but **EDIBLE.**

262. FLAT-TOP CLUB. *Clavariadelphus truncatus.* **BODY:** height 2¼–6″; yellow, orange-yellow, or tan; vertically wrinkled; top flattened, hollow; tapering to base. **FLESH:** white. **SPORES:** pale orange-red. Found scattered under conifers. **EDIBLE**

263. SPINDLE CORAL. *Clavulinopsis fusiformis.* **BODY:** height 1⅛–2¾″; deep yellow aging brown-tipped; stalks flattened and grooved or spindle-shaped; hollow, bunched at base. **FLESH:** does not snap cleanly when bent. **SPORES:** light yellow. Found scattered under hardwoods and conifers, rarely in damp open places. **NOT RECOMMENDED**

264. GRAY CORAL. *Clavulina cinerea.* **BODY:** height 1–4″; smoky or bluish-gray above to paler at base; many branched; tips rounded or pointed; often vertically grooved. **SPORES:** white. Found scattered under hardwood. **NOT RECOMMENDED**

265. AMETHYST CORAL. *Clavulina amethystina.* **BODY:** height ¾–3″; lavender above to tan-tinged below; branches many and much-divided; tips dull-pointed. **FLESH:** lavender; fragile; snap with least pressure. **SPORES:** white. Found scattered or grouped under hardwood. **EDIBILITY UNKNOWN**

266. CRESTED CORAL. *Clavulina cristata.* **BODY:** height ¾–3¼″; white to yellowish; several stalks fused and fine-branched; tips divided and sharp-pointed. **FLESH:** creamy; tough; bends without breaking. **SPORES:** white. Found singly or scattered under hardwoods and conifers or in fields. **EDIBLE**

267. CROWNED CORAL. *Clavi-corona pyxidata.* **BODY:** height 2½–5″; straw color; branches many and many-divided to "crowned" tips. **FLESH:** white; tough; bends without breaking. **SPORES:** white. Found grouped or clumped on dead wood which it decomposes. **EDIBLE**

268. ERECT CORAL. *Ramaria stricta.* **BODY:** height 1¼–3½″; tan bruising brown; many-branched from thick base, sharp-tipped. **FLESH:** tough, bends without breaking. **SPORES:** red-tan. Found scattered on dead hardwood which it decomposes. **NOT RECOMMENDED**

269. RED-TIP CORAL. *Ramaria botrytis.* **BODY:** height 3–7″; white at base to tan above with red or rosy tips; many-branched from thick base. **FLESH:** white; brittle. **SPORES:** yellow-tan. Found scattered or grouped under hardwoods and conifers. **EDIBLE**

270. CAULIFLOWER. *Sparassis crispa.* **BODY:** width 6–9″ (or more); whitish to yellowish aging tan; mass of short, flat, fanning ruffles branching from thick central stalk. **FLESH:** white; tough; fibrous. **SPORES:** whitish. Found singly under conifers and hardwoods. **EDIBLE**

PUFFBALLS. *CALVATIA.*

BODY: diameter 2½–25″ (or more); mature spores released from irregular splits of skin; sometimes has a sterile fleshy cup which persists over winter. *LYCOPERDON.* BODY: diameter ½–2′; mature spores released from a single pore at top. *BOVISTA:* BODY: diameter 1–3″; mature spores released from irregular splits of thin, brown, inner skin after white outer skin has cracked off. SPORES: *all* mature from mustard-yellow to olive, dark brown, or purple. All are found on the ground or well decayed wood and are decomposers of organic debris. Eat with caution and only in the young stage. Flesh *must* be pure white, springy, fine-spongy, with neither the appearance of gills or stem, nor insect channels—in order to be **EDIBLE.**

271. GIANT PUFFBALL. *Calvatia gigantea.* **BODY:** diameter 5–25″ (or more); white or off-white; globed; surface smooth; like fine kidskin. Found scattered. **EDIBLE**

272. PUFFBALL. *Calvatia cyathiformis.* **BODY:** diameter 3–7½″, height 4½–10′; tan or yellow-brown to purplish (rarely tinged lilac); globed or with flattened top; tapering to puckered stalklike base; surface smooth. **INTERIOR:** usually purple-brown. Found scattered. **EDIBLE**

273. BRAIN PUFFBALL. *Calvatia craniformis.* **BODY:** diameter 2½–7½″; height to 10′; tannish or gray; top rounded, often irregularly ridged; tapering to wrinkled short-stalk base; surface smooth, aging fine-scaly. **INTERIOR:** greenish-yellow. Found singly or scattered. **EDIBLE**

274. WARTED PUFFBALL. *Calvatia bovista.* **BODY:** diameter 3–7½″; height 3–7′; white with prominent flat warts and broad valleys; becoming pale yellow to brownish; globed; on thick, cylindrical base. Found singly or scattered. **EDIBLE**

275. ORANGE PUFFBALL. *Lycoperdon coloratum.* **BODY:** diameter ¾–2″; bright yellow or orange; globed, with pinched base; surface grainy. Found singly or scattered on wood on ground. **EDIBILITY UNKNOWN**

276. SPINY PUFFBALL. *Lycoperdon echinatum.* **BODY:** diameter 1–2″; white; with dense hairy spines white aging dark brown; globed. Found singly or scattered. **EDIBLE**

277. *Lycoperdon candidum.* **BODY:** ½–1″; white, spiny-warted; flattened globe pinched to narrow base. Singly, grouped, or clumped. **EDIBLE**

278. DEVIL'S SNUFFBOX. *Lycoperdon perlatum.* **BODY:** height ¾–3″, diameter ¾–1¾″; white or tan to reddish-brown; coned-spiny aging smooth-patched; globed, abruptly tapering to thick stalk-like base. Singly, grouped, clumped or in rings. **EDIBLE**

279. THE PEAR. *Lycoperdon pyriforme.* **BODY:** diameter ¾–1¾″; height ¾–1½″; white aging tannish; short-spined aging smooth; globed tapering to thick base. Found singly, scattered, or dense-clumped on rotting wood. **EDIBLE**

280. SHAGGY PUFFBALL. *Lycoperdon umbrinum.* **BODY:** diameter ¾–2″; height ¾–3½″; white; white woolly hairs shed in patches; globed, pinching to narrow base. Found scattered or loose-clumped on duff under conifers, rarely on hardwoods. **EDIBLE**

281. LITTLE BALL. *Bovista pila.* **BODY:** diameter 1¼–3¼″; white, thin, velvety outer skin cracks off exposing bronze to brown inner skin; very loosely anchored to ground; often rolling free. Found singly, scattered, or grouped. **EDIBLE**

282. *Lycogala epidendron.* This is *not* a mushroom relative; it is one of the **Slime Molds.** It is a massed group of tiny, shrimp-colored balls which quickly become metallic bronze-green to gray-brown and very fragile. The clue to the difference from Puffballs is the viscous pink liquid with which the young balls of the *Lycogala* are filled. This liquid soon becomes a gray to grayish-brown powdery substance. Often found on rotted wood. **NOT RECOMMENDED**

EARTH BALLS. BODY: firmly anchored by a dense tuft of mycelium; FLESH: dark purple or brown; white-veined when young; surrounded by a thick tough hide. Most have no opening mechanism and are dependent on insect borings or being trod upon for release of the mature spores. Found on the ground, they are decomposers of organic debris. *Warning:* many have bad reputations and *none* should be eaten.

283. WARTED EARTH BALL.
Scleroderma aurantium. **BODY:** diameter 1¼–2¾"; yellow-brown with raised circular pattern; irregularly globed. **FLESH:** gray-purple with fine white lines. Found scattered or clumped. **DANGEROUS**

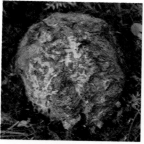

284. LARGE EARTH BALL.
Scleroderma geaster. **BODY:** diameter 2–6½"; dirty yellow to clay color aging purple-black; globed or flat-topped; usually partly underground. **FLESH:** purple; thick skin cracks into irregular lobes like earth star. Found singly or scattered. **DANGEROUS**

EARTH STARS. *GEASTRUM; ASTRAEUS.*

BODY: young, thick outer skin splits and turns back to form rays, exposing a small inner "puffball" with a central pore. Found on the ground where they are decomposers of organic debris. Though none is apparently toxic, they are **NOT RECOMMENDED.**

285. CROWNED EARTH STAR.

Geastrum coronatum. **BODY:** inner ball oval, diameter to ½", yellow-tan, pore ringed by a silky disk; 4–6" split rays, diameter to 2", thin, curving down to hold ball raised on short stem. Found singly or grouped. **NOT REC-OMMENDED**

286. EARTH STAR. *Geastrum saccatum.* **BODY:** inner ball round, diameter to ¾", dull brown, pore in a pale disk; split rays diameter to 2½", tan, felty, holding ball in an open bowl. Found scattered on damp ground or very rotted wood. **NOT RECOM-MENDED**

287. CUP AND SAUCER. *Geastrum triplex.* **BODY:** inner ball round, diameter to 1½", tan, pore in a pale disk; 4–8 split rays, diameter to 3¾", dull yellow, thick, holding ball in an irregular ring within a bowl. Found singly or grouped. **NOT RECOM-MENDED**

288. WATER MEASURER. *Astraeus hygrometricus.* **BODY:** inner ball round, diameter to 1¼", gray to tan, fuzzy, no pore but an apical tear; 7–15 split rays, diameter to 2¼", grayish, surface cracked, opening out in wet weather and closing up in dry. Found scattered on sand or dry ground. **NOT RECOMMENDED**

BIRD'S NESTS. Both are decomposers of wood or plant debris. Their tiny size eliminates their consideration as edibles.

289. BIRD'S NEST. *Crucibulum laeve.* **BODY:** height and width to ½"; tan; outside velvety, inside shiny smooth; cup-cover breaks away to expose light tan "eggs" containing the spores. Found grouped on dead twigs or bark, rarely on live wood. **NOT RECOMMENDED**

290. GROOVED BIRD'S NEST. *Cyathus striatus.* **BODY:** height to 1"; brown to dark gray; outside shaggy-hairy, inside vertically grooved; hairy cover breaks away to expose dark "eggs." Found grouped on wood debris. **NOT RECOMMENDED**

STINKHORNS. BODY: round or oval "eggs" at first. Inside the tough outer skin is a translucent gelatinous layer that covers the top of the structure, a dark gray-green or green slimy coating in which the spores are borne. The outer skin remains as a cup at the base when the stalk expands. The stalks look like hollow tubes of styrofoam, and are very fragile. The stench of the sticky slime attracts carrion flies who quickly clean it off and distribute the spores as they go. Found on the ground or on rotted wood; they are all decomposers of wood and wood debris. Most are not considered poisonous, but their fetid odor makes them unappetizing, if not inedible.

291. DOG STINKHORN. *Mutinus caninus.* **BODY:** height 2½–6″; no cap; stalk red varying in intensity, usually paler below, top slimy green; diameter to ½″, in basal cup. **EGG:** whitish, oval; length ½–1″. Found singly or scattered on ground or wood debris. **NOT RECOMMENDED**

292. GIANT STINKHORN. *Phallus ravenelii.* **BODY:** height 5–8″; cap height to 1¾″, grainy after dark-green slime is gone; stalk white, diameter to 1⅛″; in basal cup. **EGG:** off-white or pinkish, round, diameter 1–2½″. Found singly, scattered, or clumped on ground or rotting wood. **NOT RECOMMENDED**

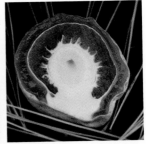

293. NETTED STINKHORN.
Dictyophora duplicata. **BODY:** height 6–8½″; cap height to 1¾″, pitted after dark gray-green slime is gone; lacy netted veil hangs from under cap-margin; stalk white, diameter to 1⅛″, in basal cup. **EGG:** flesh-color to white below, round, diameter 1¾–2¼″ Found singly or grouped on ground under dead hardwood. This picture shows total slime removal. *Phallus impudicus* is very similar but lacks the lacy skirt. Both are **NOT RECOMMENDED**

CUP FUNGI

CUP FUNGI. While some members of this diverse family have cuplike shapes, many do not. SPORES: held on exposed surfaces in microscopically small tubes or sacs, from which they are forcibly ejected through opening lid *(opercula)* or pore in the top. Most are decomposers of organic debris; some form symbiotic partnerships with higher plants, others destroy their host. *Some* are EDIBLE.

294. ORANGE PEEL. *Aleuria aurantia.* **BODY:** width ½–3½″; bright orange inside, velvety white outside; shallow cups usually distorted by crowding, fragile. **STEM:** lacking. Found grouped or clumped on ground, often in early spring as well as in summer. **EDIBLE**

295. SCARLET CUP. *Sarcoscypha coccinea.* **BODY:** width ¾–2½″; bright scarlet inside, white woolly outside; cup shallow, usually incurved. **STEM:** short. Found singly or scattered from buried sticks and twigs, during spring. **EDIBILITY UNKNOWN**

296. SUMMER CUP. *Sarcoscypha occidentalis.* **BODY:** width to ½"; red inside, whitish outside; cup very shallow. **STEM:** height varies by depth of buried sticks on which it grows. Found grouped or clumped, during midsummer. **NOT RECOMMENDED**

297. EYELASH CUP. *Scutellinia scutellata.* **BODY:** width to ½"; bright orange-red inside with dark-hairy fringed margin, dark brown and hairy outside; saucer-shaped. **STEM:** lacking. Found scattered or grouped on rotting wood or wood debris. **NOT RECOMMENDED**

298. PIG'S EAR. *Peziza badia.* **BODY:** width 1½–4"; dark brown inside, tan aging brown outside; deep cup usually distorted by crowding. **STEM:** lacking. Found scattered, grouped, or clumped on ground. When cooked, **EDIBLE;** when raw, **POISONOUS.**

299. WAVY CUP. *Peziza repanda.* **BODY:** width 1½–5"; yellow-white aging shiny chestnut inside, outside remaining yellow-white; deep cup usually distorted by crowding, often lobed or wavy. **STEM:** very short or lacking. Found clumped on rotting wood, rarely on ground. **EDIBILITY UNKNOWN**

300. BLACK GOBLET. *Urnula craterium.* BODY: cup width 1–2″; at first a closed sphere which splits open leaving margin notched and lobed; dark brown inside, black-brown and hairy outside; cup deep. STEM: height to 1¾″, black, black-woolly at base. Found grouped or clumped on ground rising from buried wood, during spring. NOT RECOMMENDED

301. DONKEY EAR. *Otidea smithii.* BODY: height 1½–2″; yellow or yellow-brown with outside paler; one side elongated, the other split to base. STEM: lacking. Found scattered or grouped on ground. EDIBILITY UNKNOWN

302. POTATO EAR. *Wynnea americana.* BODY: height 2½–4″; outside reddish-brown, inside tannish-orange; one side elongated, the other side split to base. STEM: slight or lacking; small potatolike tubers underground attached to stem. Found clustered under hardwoods. EDIBILITY UNKNOWN

303. YELLOW EAR. *Otidea onotica.* BODY: height 2½–4″; outside yellow-orange or tan-orange, inside pink-cinnamon or yellow-tan; one side elongated, the other split to base. STEM: lacking. Found scattered or clumped on ground under conifers. EDIBILITY UNKNOWN

304. WOOD STAINER. *Chlorosplenium aeruginosum.* **BODY:** width to ⅜″; blue-green; short-stemmed saucer; conspicuously staining same color the wood on which it grows. Found scattered or dense-grouped on rotted wood. **NOT RECOMMENDED**

305. YELLOW FLECKS. *Calycella citrina.* **BODY:** width to 1/₁₆″; bright yellow; flat, dense masses of tiny short-stemmed cups. Found on rotting wood or ground. **NOT RECOMMENDED**

TRUE MORELS. Found only in spring. BODY: hollow. CAPS: pitted somewhat like a sponge, with the shape and color of the pits and raised ridges good fieldmarks for distinguishing species. STEM: white to pale tan. They form symbiotic partnerships with higher plants. All are EDIBLE cooked; poisonous raw.

306. BLACK MOREL. *Morchella elata.* **CAP:** height 2–4″; top usually pointed; pits tan to blackish on squared-off ridges, elongated; cap-margin attached to stem. **STEM:** height 1–3″; almost as wide as cap, surface rough. Found scattered or grouped under hardwoods and conifers. **EDIBLE**

307. GRAY MOREL. *Morchella deliciosa.* **CAP:** height 1–2"; top rounded or a bit pointed; pits dark, gray-white on rounded ridges, irregularly round; cap-margin attached to stem. **STEM:** height 1–2"; base often enlarged. Found scattered or grouped on ground, often in grass. **EDIBLE**

308. YELLOW-MOREL. *Morchella esculenta.* **CAP:** height 2–4"; top usually blunt; pits and rounded ridges yellow-tan, irregularly round; cap-margin attached to stem. **STEM:** height 2–4"; base a bit enlarged. Found scattered or grouped on ground of open woods, orchards, grassy areas. **EDIBLE**

309. HALF-FREE MOREL. *Morchella semilibra.* **CAP:** height to 1"; round with top sharp-pointed; pits tan to almost black on thin squared-off ridges, elongated; attached to stem a short way up from margin. **STEM:** height 2–5", almost cap-width. Found scattered on ground in open woods. **EDIBLE**

FALSE MORELS
CAPS: hollow; very irregular shapes; brainlike twisted ridges, lobed or saddle-shaped. PITS: lacking. FLESH: thin; brittle. STEM: usually hollow. They form symbiotic partnerships with higher plants. All must be considered POISONOUS.

310. *Verpa conica.* **CAP:** height to 1"; usually blunt-coned; top brown, underside white; smooth or slightly radially ridged; attached to stem at top, like a thimble. **STEM:** height 1¼–2½"; whitish, scaly. Found singly or scattered on ground, during spring. **EDIBLE**

311. FALSE MOREL. *Gyromitra esculenta.* **CAP:** width 1–4"; velvety yellow-brown to red-brown; shape irregular with twisted round-ridges; cap-margin usually attached to stem. **STEM:** height to 3"; white; grooved. Found singly or scattered under conifers, during spring. **POISONOUS**

312. BROWN FALSE MOREL. *Gyromitra brunnea.* **CAP:** width 2½–6"; reddish-brown to chocolate-brown; irregularly folded and lobed or saddle-shaped. **STEM:** height 4–6"; white; hollow or cottony-stuffed; shallow-grooved or smooth. Found scattered on ground, during spring. **POISONOUS**

313. HOODED FALSE MOREL. *Gyromitra infula.* **CAP:** width 1–3" (rarely to 6"); dark brown to red-brown; simply or irregularly saddle-shaped, often wrinkled; margin *not* attached to stem. **STEM:** height 1–3"; off-white or yellowish, shallow-grooved. Found singly or scattered on ground or very rotted wood, during fall. **POISONOUS**

HELVELLA. CAP: shapes may be saddlelike or cupped. Character of stem and time of fruiting are important for species identification. They form symbiotic partnerships with higher plants. *All* must be considered POISONOUS

314. ELFIN SADDLE. *Helvella crispa.* **CAP:** width ½–2″; white to pale cream; saddle-shaped or lobed. **STEM:** height 1–2½″; cap-color; irregularly deeply fluted. Found singly, scattered, or grouped on ground or very rotted wood. Grows during period from August to October. **POISONOUS**

315. SMOOTH-STEM SADDLE. *Helvella elastica.* **CAP:** width ¼–2″; tan, pale gray, or brownish; saddle-shaped or lobed. **STEM:** height 1–3″; cream to tan; not fluted; slender. Found singly or grouped on ground. Grows during period from August to October. **POISONOUS**

316. EARLY SADDLE. *Helvella stevensii.* **CAP:** ½–2″; tan; saddle-shaped to three-lobed. **STEM:** height ½–3″; cream; not fluted; base a bit enlarged. Found scattered or grouped under hardwoods, during early summer. **POISONOUS**

317. GRAY VEINED-CUP. *Helvella griseoalba.* **CUP:** width ¾–2¼″; gray; forking light thick veins extend down stem; cup flattens with age. **STEM:** height none to 1″; white; deeply fluted. Found scattered or grouped under hardwoods and fruit trees, during spring and early summer. **NOT RECOMMENDED**

318. BROWN VEINED-CUP. *Helvella acetabulum.* **CUP:** width 1–4″; inside light to dark smoky brown, outside pale cream at cup-base with forking veins extending down stem. **STEM:** height none to 1″; cream; deeply fluted. Found scattered to grouped under hardwoods, during spring and early summer. **NOT RECOMMENDED**

319. LITTLE SPATULA. *Spathularia flavida.* **BODY:** height 1–2¼″; yellow or yellow-tan tough little ruffles in one dimension around brown or dark tan coned hollow stalk. Found grouped on ground. **EDIBILITY UNKNOWN**

320. GOLD-HEAD. *Leotia lubrica.* **BODY:** height 1¼–2½″, head width to ⅜″; translucent yellow, golden tan, rarely green-tinged; all parts very slippery-slimy. Found grouped or clumped on ground or rotting wood or wood debris, which it decomposes. **EDIBILITY UNKNOWN**

321. GREEN-HEAD. *Leotia atrovirens.* **BODY:** height ¼–2″; head width to ¼″; all parts green aging slippery-slimy. Found singly or grouped on ground; it is a decomposer of wood or wood debris. **EDIBILITY UNKNOWN**

322. FILLED CUP. *Galiella rufa.* **BODY:** width 1–1½″; top dark brown, closed at first; opens to a pinkish-tan to red-brown shallow saucer; rubbery-gelatinous when fresh, drying wrinkled and leathery. **STEM:** very short or lacking. Found scattered or clumped on ground from buried wood. **EDIBILITY UNKNOWN**

323. BLACK SAUCER. *Bulgaria inquinans.* **BODY:** unopened globe, width to ¾″, rusty, velvety, rubbery-gelatinous; opened, a black shining saucer to 1½″ across; base very short, thick. Found grouped on dead hardwoods, often oaks. **EDIBILITY UNKNOWN**

324. WOOD BALL. *Daldinia concentrica.* **BODY:** diameter to 1¾"; velvety brown quickly turning black; interior concentrically zoned black, solid, brittle-hard. Found singly or scattered on dead hardwoods. **NOT RECOMMENDED**

325. BLACK KNOT. *Apiosporina morbosa.* **BODY:** length 1¼–8"; dark green-brown quickly turning black; solid brittle-hard. Found surrounding and killing branches of live cherry and chokecherry. **NOT RECOMMENDED**

326. DEAD MAN'S FINGERS. *Xylaria polymorpha.* **CLUB:** height 1¾–3½"; dark gray quickly turning black; fine-pitted; interior pure white, woody; clubs single or branched. Found singly or clumped on dead hardwood or from buried roots. **NOT RECOMMENDED**

327. BLACK ANTLERS. *Xylaria hypoxylon.* **CLUB:** height 1½–3¼"; grayish quickly turning black; single clubs branching above to sharp points; corky. Found grouped on dead hardwoods. **NOT RECOMMENDED**

RUSTS.
Parasites on living plants. Most are inconspicuous but a few have more obvious structures, usually an orange or bright yellow group of warts or a cluster of drooping strands.

328. CEDAR-APPLE RUST.
Gymnosporangium juniperi-virginianae. **BODY:** diameter to 1¼"; in rainy weather bright tawny-orange, clusters of drooping gelatinous tongues; in dry weather, a small, round, brown gall. Found scattered on healthy cedars which are not badly harmed, but cause disease on leaves of nearby apple trees. **EDIBILITY UNKNOWN**

FUNGI FOUND ON OTHER FUNGI

FUNGI ON FUNGI.
Parasites that use their relatives for sustenance. Of those we include, three are gilled mushrooms and three—Cordyceps and Hypomyces—are Cup fungi.

329. *Asterophora lycoperdoides.*
CAP: mature width to ⅝"; tiny white balls at first, developing short stems and dingy whitish caps thickly brown-powdered. **GILLS:** attached; distant, when present. When lacking, the dense powder on the cap is a secondary type of viable spore for the survival of the species. **SPORES:** white on gills; brown on cap. Found grouped on aging Black Russula, occasionally on some *Lactarii.* **EDIBILITY UNKNOWN**

330. *Asterophora parasiticus.* **CAP:**
width to ½"; silky white to gray aging brown-powdered; knobbed. **STEM:** very slender, usually curved. (See *Asterophora lycoperdoides.*) Found in crowded groups and clumps on aging Short Stem Russula and some white *Lactarii.* **EDIBILITY UNKNOWN**

331. ORANGE CLUB. *Cordyceps militaris.* **BODY:** height 1–2"; head width to ¼"; yellowish-orange with orange dots on surface. Found singly or widely scattered, growing from buried insect larvae. **NOT RECOMMENDED**

332. NAIL HEAD. *Cordyceps capitata.* **BODY:** height 1–3½", head width to ¾"; brown to blackish with olive-yellowish stalk. Found grouped on ground, rising from a subterranian fungus (e.g. a False Truffle or *Elaphomyces* sp.). **NOT RECOMMENDED**

333. BEAD BLANKET. *Hypomyces lactifluorum.* **BODY:** brilliant orange; beadlike thin coating usually covering all of host. Because it causes all degrees of distortion and abortion of the mushroom itself, it is usually difficult to be sure of the species on which it is growing, usually one of the *Russulas* or *Lactarii.* **DANGEROUS**

334. *Psathyrella epimyces.* **CAP:** width ¾–2¼"; dingy white; silky-thready; some with marginal veil remnants. **FLESH:** white. **GILLS:** shallow-attached; close; gray aging brown-black; edges white. **STEM:** height ¾–3"; mealy cap-color; base white-ringed with veil remnants. **SPORES:** almost black. From one to seven are found on cap of host, usually the Gray Ink-Cap and Shaggy Mane. **POISONOUS**

Index

Artist's Palette (*Ganoderma applanatum*), 93:208
Asterophora (genus), 33
   A. lycoperdoides, 126:329
   A. parasiticus, 126:330
Astraeus (genus), 30, 114
   A. hygrometricus (Water Measurer), 115:288
Auricularia, 29
Auriscalpium (genus), 29
   A. vulgare (Stemmed Ear), 106:255

Balsam Russula (*Russula abietina*), 59:86
Bark Mycena (*Mycena corticola*), 64:104
Barlocher, F., 10
Bead Blanket (*Hypomyces lactifluorum*), 127:333
Bear (*Lentinellus ursinus*), 65:109
Bear's Head (*Hericium ramosum*), 106:257
Big Rosette (*Grifola gigantea*), 97:220
Birch Conk (*Piptoporus betulinus*), 89:195
Bird's Nest (*Crucibulum laeve*), 115:289
Bitter Bolete (*Tylopilus felleus*), 89:193
Bitter Milk-Cap (*Lactarius necator*), 55:61
Bitter Panellus (*Panellus stipticus*), 66:113
Bjerkandera (genus), 26
   B. adusta (Scorched Bracket), 92:202
   B. fumosa, 92:202
Black Antlers (*Xylaria hypoxylon*), 125:327
Black Foot (*Polyporus elegans*), 97:223

Black Goblet (*Urnula Craterium*), 119:300
Black Jelly (*Exidia glandulosa*), 104:247
Black Knot (*Apiosporina morbosa*), 125:325
Black Morel (*Morchella elata*), 120:306
Black Saucer (*Bulgaria inquinans*), 124:323
Black-spored mushrooms, 24–25
Black Stem (*Polyporus picipes*), 97:224
Black Velvet (*Phellodon niger*), 107:260
Blackening Russula (*Russula densifolia*), 57:75
Bleeder (*Mycena haematopa*), 63:100
Blue-Gills (*Clitocybe nuda*), 48:37
Blue Milk-Cap *(Lactarius indigo),* 55:67
Blue Stainer (*Gyroporus cyanescens*), 88:192
Blue-Stem (*Leptonia asprella*), 72:131
Blunt Antlers (*Calocera viscosa*), 104:250
Blushing Lepiota (*Lepiota americana*), 39:11
Body form, 14
Boletes, 10, 25, 85
Boletus (genus), 10, 25–30, 85
   B. chromapes (Painted Bolete), 87:189
   B. luridus (Lurid Bolete), 87:188
Bovista (genus), 30, 110
   B. pila (Little Ball), 112:281
Brain Puffball (*Calvatia craniformis*), 111:273
Brick Top (*Naematoloma sublateritium*), 81:168
Broad-Gills (*Tricholomopsis playphylla*), 43:23

Brown Amanita (*Amanita brunnescens*), 38:7

Brown Crust (*Phellinus punctatus*), 99:229

Brown False Morel (*Gyromitra brunnea*), 122:312

Brown-Spined Little Flame (*Pholiota erinaceella*), 76:148

Brown-spored mushrooms, 23–24

Brown Veined-Cup (*Helvella acetabulum*), 123:318

Bulbed Agaric (*Agaricus sylvicola*), 80:164

Bulgaria (genus), 32
  B. inquinans (Black Saucer), 124:323

Calocera (genus), 29
  C. cornea (Sharp Antlers), 104:248
  C. viscosa (Blunt Antlers), 104:250

Calvatia (genus), 30, 110
  C. bovista (Warted Puffball), 111:274
  C. craniformis (Brain Puffball), 111:273
  C. cyathiformis (Puffball), 110:272
  C. gigantea (Giant Puffball), 110:271

Calycella (genus), 31
  C. citrina (Yellow Flecks), 120:305

Cantharellus (genus), 20, 45
  C. cibarius (Golden Chanterelle), 45:29
  C. cinnabarinus (Vermillion Chanterelle), 46:30
  C. tubaeformis (Trumpet), 46:31

Cap attachment, 17

Cap form, 14

Carved Amanita (*Amanita solitaria*), 38:8

Cauliflower (*Sparassis crispa*), 109:270

Cedar-Apple Rust (*Gymnosporanglum juniperi-virginianae*), 126:328

Cerrena (genus), 28
  C. unicolor, 100:233

Chalk-Top (*Leucoagaricus naucinus*), 10, 14, 42:20

Chameleon (*Russula chamaeleontina*), 59:85

Chlorophyllum (genus), 19, 39
  C. molybdites (Green-Gills), 41:17

Chlorosplenium (genus), 31
  C. aeruginosum (Wood Stainer), 120:304

Chocolate Shelf (*Gloeophyllum sepiarium*), 99:231

Chroogomphus (genus), 25
  C. rutilus (Shiny Nail), 84:179
  C. vinicolor (Little Nail), 84:178

Cinnamon-spored mushrooms, 23–24

Citrine Amanita (*Amanita citrina*), 36:2

Clavariadelphus (genus), 30
  C. pistillaris (Indian Club), 107:261
  C. truncatus (Flat Top Club), 108:262

Clavicorona (genus), 30
  C. pyxidata (Crowned Coral), 109:267

Clavulina (genus), 30
  C. amethystina (Amethyst Coral), 108:265
  C. cinerea (Gray Coral), 108:264
  C. cristata (Crested Coral), 108:266

Clavulinopsis (genus), 30
  C. fusiformis (Spindle Coral), 108:263

Climacodon (genus), 26, 30
  C. borealis, 90:197
  C. septentrionale (Toothed Bracket), 107:259

Clinker (*Phellinus tremulae*), 95:214

G. *floccosus* (Scaly Funnel), 46:32

Granular Bolete (*Suillus granulatus*), 85:183

Gray Coral (*Clavulina cinerea*), 108:264

Gray-Cup (*Aleurodiscus oakesii*), 100:234

Gray Entoloma (*Entoloma lividum*), 71:128

Gray Ink-Caps (*Coprinus atramentarius*), 8, 82:170, 127:334

Gray Morel (*Morchella deliciosa*), 121:307

Gray Ringless Amanita (*Amanita vaginata*), 38:9

Gray Veined-Cup (*Helvella griseoalba*), 123:317

Green Crust (*Russula virescens*), 59:87

Green-Gills (*Chlorophyllum molybdites*), 10, 41:17

Green-Head (*Leotia atrovirens*), 124:321

Green Russula (Russula aeruginea), 60:88

Grifola (genus), 27

G. *frondosa* (Hen of the Woods), 96:219

G. *gigantea* (Big Rosette), 97:220

Grooved Bird's Nest (*Cyathus striatus*), 115:290

Ground Funnel (*Coltricia perennis*), 98:226

Gymnopilus (genus), 23, 74

G. *luteofolius* (Rusty Clusters), 77:150

G. *sapineus* (Conifer Gymnopilus), 77:151

Gymnosporangium (genus), 33

G. *juniperi-virginianae* (Cedar-Apple Rust), 126:328

Gyrodon (genus), 25

G. *merulioides* (Veined Bolete), 85:180

Gyromitra (genus), 32

G. *brunnea* (Brown False Morel), 122:312

G. *esculenta* (False Morel), 122:311

G. *infula* (Hooded False Morel), 122:313

Gyrophorus (genus), 26, 85

G. *cyanescens* (Blue Stainer), 88:192

Hairy Wax-Cap (*Hygrophorus russula*), 52:55

Half-Free Morel (*Morchella semilibra*), 121:309

Hapalopilus (genus), 27

H. *nidulans* (Nest Bracket), 95:215

Hebeloma (genus), 23

H. *crustuliniforme* (Poison Pie), 72:139

Hedgehog (*Dentinum repandum*), 105:253

Helvella (genus), 32, 123

H. *acetabulum* (Brown Veined-Cup), 123:318

H. *crispa* (Elfin Saddle), 127:314

H. *elastica* (Smooth-Stem Saddle), 123:318

H. *griseoalba* (Gray Veined-Cup), 123:317

H. *stevensii* (Early Saddle), 123:316

Hen of the Woods (*Grifola frondosa*), 96:219

Hericium (genus), 30

H. *coralloides* (Large White Coral), 106:256

H. *erinaceus* (Medusa's Head), 107:258

H. *ramosum* (Bear's Head), 106:257

Hirschioporus (genus), 26

H. *abietina*, 92:205

H. *pargamenus* (Parchment Bracket), 92:205

138

Tawny Ringless Amanita (*Amanita fulva*), 38:9
Thelephora (genus), 28
  T. terrestris, 101:238
Thelephores, 28, 100–101
Tiger (*Lentinus tigrinus*), 65:106
Tinderwood (*Fomes fomentarius*), 94:212
Toothed Bracket (*Climacodon septentrionale*), 107:259
Toothed fungi, 29–30, 105–107
Toothed Jelly (*Pseudohydnum gelatinosum*), 102:240
Torn fiberhead (Inocybe lacera), 78:158
Train Wrecker (*Lentinus lepideus*), 64:105
Trametes (genus), 26
T. suaveolens (Sweet Trametes), 89:194
Tremella (genus), 29
  T. concrescens (White Blanket), 103:246
  T. foliacea (Leafy Jelly), 103:243
  T. fuciformis (White Tremella), 103:244
  T. lutescens (Pale Witch's Butter), 102:241
  T. mesenterica (Golden Witch's Butter), 102:241
  T. reticulata (Hollow-Lobed Tremella), 103:245
Tremellodendron (genus), 29
  T. pallidum (Flat-Stem Jelly), 104:249
Tricholoma (genus), 20, 43
Tricholomopsis (genus), 20, 43
  T. playphylla (Broad-Gills), 43:23
  T. rutilans (Red-Tuft), 43:22
Trumpet (*Cantharellus tubaeformis*), 46:31
Tubed fungi, 25–28, 85–100
Tubes, 16
Turkey Tail (*Coriolus versicolor*), 91:199

Tylopilus (genus), 26, 85
  T. felleus (Bitter Bolete), 89:193
Tyromyces (genus), 26
  T. albellus, 90:196

Urnula (genus), 31
  U. craterium (Black Goblet), 119:300

Veined Bolete (*Gyrodon merulioides*), 85:180
Velvet Milk-Cap (*Lactarius vellereus*), 54:68
Velvet Peg (*Paxillus atrotomentosus*), 79:159
Velvet Psathyrella (*Psathyrella velutina*), 81:167
Velvet Russula (*Russula mariae),* 59:84
Velvet Stem (*Flammulina velutipes*), 8, 62:97
Velvet Top (*Phaeolus schweinitzii*), 94:210
Vermillion Chanterelle (*Cantharellus cinnabarinus*), 46:30
Vermillion Pluteus (*Pluteus aurantiorugosus*), 70:126
Vermillion Wax-Gill (*Hygrophorus coccineus*), 51:49
Verpa (genus), 31
  V. conica, 122:310
Violet Cortinarius (*Cortinarius alboviolaceus*), 73:134
Volvariella (genus), 22, 69
  V. bombycina (Ermine Cloak), 69:121
  V. pusillia (Little Ermine Cloak), 69:123
  V. volvacea (Sooty Cloak), 69:122

Warted Earth Ball (*Scleroderma aurantium*), 113:283
Warted Puffball (*Calvatia bovista*), 111:274